STREET BOY

Fletch Brown

Gabriel
Publishing

PO Box 1047
Waynesboro, GA 30830 USA
Email: postmaster@omlit.om.org

Copyright 1980, by Fletch Brown

First Gabriel Publishing printing, 2001.

ISBN: 1-884543-64-2

Cover design: Paul Lewis

Printed in Colombia.

1

Old Lady Columna was standing too close to the fruit rack. "Meatman" leaned against the cashbox, always touching it even when he cut meat. With the patience of an expert hunter, Jaime Jorka watched, waited, knowing sooner or later someone would get careless and he would have his chance to steal. The Quinta Market in Quiapo, Manila, the Philippines, was a big place, but it was home to Jaime.

The market was in a large, shed like building on the Pasig River nearly under the Quezon Boulevard Bridge in the heart of the city. Independent merchants of bread, fish, fruit, meat, copra, cloth, vegetables, pottery, and everything else needed by the teeming populace of the city displayed their wares in a multitude of stalls filling all available space. The noise was oppressive. Merchants hawking wares, customers arguing prices, wandering hucksters selling treats, friends greeting friends — all was done at the top of the voice. That day the heat hung over the market and the building smelled strongly of fish, horses, and garbage.

Jaime had been stealing from the merchants for most of his thirteen years. Today he felt lucky. He had better be. Yesterday he and Rio Rodriquez had worked the Frisco Market in San Francisco del Monte and they had not got a thing. He had been too ashamed to go home. Mama would yell at him and small sister would tease him, and he would hit small sister, and then Mama would yell some more. So Jaime had slept under the newspapers with Rio in a box that Rio called home.

"Rio! That tall one, at the shine box. You hit him, I grab his wallet. Go!" The tall, dark-haired man had just had a shoeshine and was paying the boy. They double-teamed him with skill born of long practice. He did not have a chance. Rio bumped into him and yelled. Jaime grabbed the wallet out of his hand, and the two melted into the crowd. Jaime met the man's eyes for one brief moment, and then he was gone. They did not even try for the coins that were spilled; others could take care of them. Now they just wanted to get away.

After turning a few corners, Jaime slowed down and looked for Rio. He was not in sight, so Jaime slipped a few coins out of the wallet into his pocket. He was holding the wallet tightly closed and nonchalantly looking at the design on the outside when Rio caught up.

"How much?" asked Rio.

"Don' know," Jaime answered. "Let's go back to the box, then we see." He made a big show of holding the wallet closed. *Rio's kinda dumb,* Jaime thought. He could get him to do or believe almost anything. *Well, that's the only kinda friends you can have in this business. If they're too smart they take you before you can take them.*

"Hey! Where's your name thing?"

Jaime reached for his neck. He had carved his name in a small piece of wood and had hung it around his neck. Now it was gone. He stopped and whirled toward the market. He stood poised for only a moment, then relaxed, shrugged, and turned back on his way.

"I sure not goin' back to look for it now. If I want another one, I carve another one. Ha." It was forgotten.

Rio's box was on the outskirts of Tondo, one of the large squatter areas of Manila. He had no family. He had no home. The large packing crate was all he had. It was located on the edge of Tondo near the stores and shops where he could steal, or near the restaurants whose garbage cans he could raid.

When they got to the box they made sure no one was watching, and they opened the wallet.

"Three hundred pesos, even!" Jaime counted. "We split it even, OK?"

"OK, that's good."

"Here's your half, one hundred twenty-five pesos. I tell you what, I give you five pesos extra an' I keep the wallet."

"Wait a minute!" Rio's eyes narrowed. "How come you get so generous! Huh? Why the extra five? You try to pull somethin'?"

"No, Rio, I just like you. Besides, I think you want the wallet so I buy it from you. OK?" *You dumb-dumb,* Jaime thought, *I cheat you out of twenty and you argue over five.*

3

"OK. I go get something to eat now."

"Fine. I think I go home. See you tomorrow."

On the way home Jaime studied the wallet. It had a funny design on one side. It looked like a fish with some strange letters in it. There was an *I*, then an X, then an *O* with a line through it, a Y, then a letter that looked like a Z with an extra wiggle in it. There was something familiar about it. Jaime was sure he had seen it someplace before, but he could not remember where.

He walked deeper and deeper into the squatters' area of Tondo, heading for the western side near the docks where his father sometimes worked. Some of the shanties he passed were quite substantial, made of wood with flattened oil cans for roof and siding. Some had corrugated metal sheets for roofs, others were no more than cardboard walls with canvas tops. Babies, naked but for a shirt, played in the dirt and mud of the roads. Swarms of children ran and shrieked at their games. Dead-eyed women stared unseeing from doorways, the hopelessness of their poverty etched in their faces. Jaime had smelled the dirt and garbage and open toilets too long even to notice them. Besides, he had other things on his mind. He was doing some very careful figuring.

He had a total of 195 pesos. If he gave it all to his mama, his papa would beat it out of her and spend it on drink. Worse, she would think he had more than 195 pesos and scream at him to give her the rest. *So, I'll give her about fifty*, Jaime thought, *then when she screams at me for the rest I will give her another twenty, maybe, and hide the rest. But if Papa beats it out of her I can still give her fifty more, and she can buy food when he's drunk. If he don't I'll give it to her tomorrow or the next day. Buy myself some peace, that's what I'll do.*

But maybe someday I'll be a big man and have a big gang, and we will raid the docks and other places and make big money. Then I can relax. I'll buy me some cars and girls and bash in Papa's drunken face and buy Mama nice clothes and slap her face when she yells at me and kick A'te Marie and twist Herminia's ear until she begs me to —

"Jaime, you lazy, no good, bad boy! Where you been?" Mama's screeching, high-pitched voice broke his thoughts. He was home.

The Jorka shanty was a little more substantial than most. Though still a rude shelter by most standards, it was all wood and tin with no cardboard. Jaime had lived here as long as he could remember. Some of his earliest memories were of helping Papa carry home pieces of wood and tin to add on to the size and fix broken parts. Its one glass window, a luxury seldom found in Tondo, made Jaime proud. He remembered how he stole it from the overturned lumber truck. He had grabbed it from the pile and run all the way home with it, afraid someone would catch him and make him give it back. No one was home when he got there, so he put it into the cardboard wall they had had then, fixing it in place with some boards. Papa was too drunk to notice when he got home and all Mama said was, "You could have sold it for money!" But they left it there.

Bit by bit Jaime had built up the wall with planks of wood and pieces of tin until the window could not be removed without tearing down the whole wall. He had built a little lean-to on the back of the shack, a small place he could crawl into to be alone with his thoughts and dreams. Jaime Jorka was very clever with his hands and very clever with his mind. And he had a burning desire, hot within him, to get out of those slums.

Mama was still screaming at him. With one hand she held baby Florita on her hip, with the other she reached for him, clutching and grabbing at the air.

"You better have some money or I kick your face."

"Sure, Mama. Sure, Mama. I got some money. Why you think I came home? To play with my sweet little sister, Herminia? Look! I got fifty-five pesos."

"You got more, I bet you. Hand it over!"

"Mama! Would I ever cheat you?"

"You bet you would." She grabbed him with her free hand and started to shake him. "Come on now! Come on now! All of it!"

"OK, OK. Stop shaking me. Here's the rest." He gave her twenty-three pesos more. "I can't fool you, can I, Mama? You're too smart."

"Here, you take care Florita. I gotta go quick and buy

food before your papa comes home." She thrust his baby sister at him and hurried down the street to the same market Jaime had just come from.

Stupid. Stupid. Jaime thought. *More stupid even than Rio.* "I hope you don't grow up to be so stupid," he said, addressing the baby. "But I suppose you will die of a rat bite and never grow up at all. Maybe you be better off."

He went into their shanty and put the baby in the crib he had made for her. They had had a real crib once, but Papa had hocked it. So Jaime made another one out of lumber he stole from the docks. He ducked down into his little lean-to and, making sure no one was looking, opened his secret hiding place and put the wallet and money in, and took out a magazine.

He rolled back on the mattress he had made from shredded paper, opening the magazine. He was thankful he could read. It had been fun going to school. That was before Papa started to drink so much and they could afford it. But he could read and was good at arithmetic, two skills he knew he needed to get up out of life in the shanty. He read everything he could get his hands on and stored it all away in his sharp, retentive mind.

He leafed through the magazine, and — wait! There it was! That symbol, like the fish, with the strange letters in it. He looked at the advertisement closely. It read: "Jesus Christ, God's Son, Savior. That's what those letters stand for. They are in Greek, a strange language from halfway around the world. But Jesus isn't halfway around the world. He is as close as a prayer. Jesus loves you and He wants to help you. Will you let Him? Write to —"

Ha! If Jesus wanted to help me, He better send money. That's the only help I can use. Money. Money. It's the only thing that will ever get me out of this shack, out of this neighborhood, and out of this life. You can talk all you want, but it is only money that will ever get you anywhere.

"Jaime! I heard Mama tell you to take care of Florita! You do it!" Marie yelled at him from the shack. *Fat chance, you lazy good-for-nothing* he thought. *Florita's your responsibility when Mama's not home. I'm not going to let you get out of it, no matter what Mama said.*

"You do it! You do it or I tell Mama!" Her voice went up another couple of notches. Jaime put away his magazine and charged out of his lean-to and into the shack to see what was wrong. The baby was dressed like all babies in Tondo, a small shirt and a bare bottom. Now she needed cleaning up and Marie did not want to.

"Ooh, A'te Marie, my big sister. I am so sorry your hands are dead. It is too bad you can do nothing."

"Lazy pig! Bah!"

"Lazy pig? How much money did you bring home today?" Jaime knew that would infuriate her. It was a thinly-veiled insult.

"Monkey! Pig! Dog! Pig!! Pig. Pig, pig pigpigpig!!"

"Oh! I'm sorry. It is your head that is dead, not your

hands. You are screeching just like Mama now."

"Jaime's Mama! Jaime's Mama!" small sister Herminia taunted as she came in. Jaime started to kick at her, but changed his mind. Marie would tell Mama about that.

No wonder Papa drinks, he thought. *With all the noise and yelling it's enough to make anyone want to — No! I will not think that! No matter what! I will never get like Papa. That is stupid. And I am not stupid! I'm not, not, not, not stupid! I'm smart and I am gonna get out of here.*

Rage and frustration started to boil inside him, knotting his stomach and blinding his eyes. *This stinking hole, those shrieking voices —*

"You watch her. I'm going out!" he yelled at both sisters as he slammed into the streets. He blundered along noticing neither scene nor person. Hot tears of rage filled his eyes and his teeth ground together. *I'll show them,* he thought, *I'll show them. I'll make it big. I'll get out of this mess. Some day they will call me Mister Jorka. I'll have cars and money and—* He tempered his rage with dreams of future glory until it became just a dull ache deep inside of him. *Don't let it go,* he thought. *Don't ever let that ache go away if you ever do you will end up like Papa, a drunk with a no-good wife and a bunch of kids living in a junk shack.* No. Not for him. Jaime Jorka was better than that. He would make it. He did not need anybody!

Suddenly he thought of the advertisement about Jesus. He started to laugh. *Ha! How would Jesus help me? Rain down money from the sky? Drive a new car to my door? No way!* Jaime threw back his head and laughed and laughed.

"Hello." A voice brought him back to reality. Jaime found himself looking straight into the eyes of the man he had just robbed.

2

An alarm bell of shock went through Jaime, snapping him to full attention.

"You were laughing so much you almost bumped me. You must be very happy."

Jaime's calm air belied the coilspring tenseness inside of him. He was bunched like a cat, but he forced himself to be calm. One false move and he was done.

"I was thinking of something very funny, Mr. American."

"Is my accent that bad?" The man laughed. "I have been here two years and I thought my Tagalog was pretty good."

Why doesn't he grab me? Jaime thought. He was careful to stay out of arm's reach and to be sure there was room to run, that he was not blocked from escape.

"Your Tagalog is better than some who have been here for ten years."

"You speak as a gentleman. You don't talk like most street boys."

Jaime laughed. "Now you are the gentleman." *Watch it!* he told himself. *This isn't one of the stupid ones.* "I have to go, you will excuse me. Na'nay and Ta'tay are expecting me soon." Jaime wondered if he understood the words.

"Yes. You must obey your parents," the man answered. "May I walk with you? It isn't very often that I get to talk to a street boy as smart as you. Most of them act rather stupid. My name is Art. What's yours?" Art put his hands in his pockets, a motion not lost on Jaime. The man could not make a quick grab at him that way.

"If you wish. My name is Jaime." He started toward home.

Art fell in beside Jaime. "What were you laughing at?"

Now what does he want? Jaime could not quite make the man out. He felt sure, now, that Art had not recognized him, but if he had not, why was he walking with him? What did he want? There was something different about Art. Maybe it would pay to talk to him. If he could not get any more money out of him, at least he could learn something.

"I laughed at an ad I saw in a magazine." *Don't tell any more lies than you have to.*

"What did it say?"

"It said Jesus wanted to help me. Ha. How can He help me? I see Him in the church, hanging on the cross. He's dead. He can't help me."

Art almost stumbled, looked skyward, smiled, and looked back at Jaime in wonder.

"How can He help me?" Jaime challenged.

"Many ways," Art answered calmly.

"Huh? What you mean?" Sparks came back into Jaime's eyes. "He gonna give me money? That's what you need to get you out of this." He waved his arm at the slum neighborhood they had entered. "Money. Plenty money. Look at me! How can I get money unless I st—" *Watch, you idiot!* he thought. "Well, how can I get it?"

"You want to get out of here pretty bad, don't you?"

"Yes! And I'm gonna!"

"Jaime, I have a deal to offer you — but, no, you wouldn't take it."

"What you mean?"

"You wouldn't believe me."

"Try me."

"How would you like to get out of here for a whole week, for free? There is a camp out in Bataan we would like to send you to. You get all you can eat, three meals a day. We have sports, swimming, crafts, and you learn how Jesus can help you."

"You're right. I don't believe you."

"It's true."

"What is it? A trap? Sure you feed me. You put me in a good bed. And when I wake up next day — ha! —I'm in the army! No, thank you. I wanna get out of here, but I wanna get out my way. Keep your army trap."

"No, no, Jaime. There is someone who wants you out of here just as much as you want to get out. He loves you and wants to help you."

"You mean Jesus? Ha!"

"I know you don't believe me, but I tell you what. You know where Bonifacio school is, don't you? OK. Tomorrow, late afternoon, you come there and watch for a Pantranco Company bus. There are a bunch of fellows just coming back from camp. You meet them and ask them about it. See what they say. OK?"

"I don't know." Jaime was very quiet.

"I'll be there, too, if you have any questions. See you tomorrow. Good-bye, Jaime." Art walked away. He turned and waved once. Jaime stood and watched him until he was out of sight.

He slowly walked toward home. Art *was* different. *I think he's telling the truth,* Jaime pondered, *but why? What is this? There must be more to it. People don't do things like that unless they want something. It's crazy. No one ever been like that to me before. I go over to the school tomorrow and see. I betcha I find something fishy.*

He drew up short of the shack. Mama was home, cooking some rice and vegetables. He would wait. Let them eat first. He would take what was left. He could always steal some more if there was not enough.

Art was right. There was a big load of boys who got off the bus the next day — the happiest, cheeriest bunch of street boys Jaime had ever seen. They were singing some song he had never heard as the bus pulled up, laughing and shouting in the best of spirits. Each boy was carrying something. There were kites, carvings, papers, and all had little cloth sacks. Jaime looked for a familiar face and finally spotted one. It was Ernesto — Little Mouse, they used to call him, and rightly so.

"Hey! Ernesto. Where you been on the bus, huh?"

"Hi, Jaime. You gonna go to camp too? You'll like it."

"Don't know. What kinda camp is it?"

"It's a good camp."

"I mean, they treat you OK there? No trap like the army or jail or somethin'?"

"No. No! It's good! You should go, Jaime, you should go!"

"Why? 'Cause they give you everything. Food! All you can, eat! And clothes, and books, and fun, and kites." He laughed and held up all the things he had. Ernesto looked square into Jaime's eyes. "They give you life!"

"Yeah, thanks." Jaime turned away. For some reason that last remark made him feel uncomfortable. *Ernesto's changed,* Jaime thought, *he ain't "Little Mouse" any more. There something different, something like — something like Art! But that's silly' Art's a—*

"Hey, Jaime, catch!" He turned just in time to catch the orange Art threw to him. "I didn't lie to you after all, did I?" Art laughed as Jaime bit off part of the rind and began to suck the juice.

"Yeah. That Ernesto, he said you give him everything. He said you give him life. What's he mean?"

Art's smile took in the whole world. "Why don't you come and find out for yourself?" he said quietly. He looked Jaime straight in the eye just as Ernesto had. "I got work to do. See you later."

Once again Jaime stood and watched as Art walked out of sight.

Rio bought a basketball. Though he needed food and clothes, he had bought a basketball with the money they had stolen from Art. Jaime had scrounged a couple of boards and a barrel hoop and nailed them, rather precariously, to a light pole. Their "court" was only about ten feet wide, between two buildings, and about fifteen feet to the street. The pole was on the edge of a bank that led down to one of the small streams, no more than open sewers, running through Tondo. If the ball ever missed the small backboard it landed in the stinking mud of the stream. Rio loved that ball. Every time it went into the mud he would shout and yell at the one who let it go, carefully pick it out of the stink, and wipe it on his shirt. Soon he was smelling worse than the stream.

"Hey! You're a real stinker!" Jaime mocked him when he missed a shot.

"That ball's a stinker when it don't go in the hoop," one of the other boys chided.

"I gonna take this stinking shirt off!" Rio finally decided.

They would play a game something like "rotation." Whoever got the rebound would have to dribble back to the street and then come in and make his pass at the hoop. No score was kept unless they made up teams. Even then there were more arguments and yelling over the count than anything else.

Jaime was smaller than most boys his age, but he more than made up for it by his quickness and intense drive. He always had to show that he was better. He always had to excel at everything he did. If he did not excel at something, he would not do it. The drive came from somewhere deep inside him. He never stopped to think about where it came from, but he knew it was the only thing that was going to get him out of Tondo, so he nurtured it.

Pretty soon there would be more dirt than clean on Rio's shirt, and the ball would get too slippery to handle. Then they would break and go about two blocks to a water faucet where the local people drew their water, and wash off the ball, their hands, and Rio's shirt, and return to play.

One day, after about the third such trip, Jaime left them and headed toward the Quinta Market.

"I'm getting too hungry. I think I go see if I can't find something to eat."

"Yeah, sure. Just don't find it before someone loses it."

"Ha. Very funny. If I find something good, I bring it back."

"Now who's funny!"

His hunger was just an excuse. Jaime, like all street boys, never got enough to eat, so hunger was no stranger to him. Actually, it had been several days since he had last talked to Art, and he hoped to find him at the market. He was in luck.

"Catch!" Art's typical greeting, and orange, 'caught' him just outside the market. Jaime tried not to show his pleasure at meeting his strange new friend, but he had some

17

things he had been thinking about and he wanted to talk. Soon they were leaning against the wall of the market deep in conversation.

"Now, when I ask you why you give me an orange, you say, 'Because I love you.' But that cannot be. You want something. Even you, Mr. American, Mr. Missionary, you want something." Jaime's suspicion had been nurtured by long years of hard living.

"Yes, I want something. I want a better life for you. I want to see you get out of here."

"But, why, why! It ain't natural!"

"Jaime, it is as simple as this: Christ said, 'Love others as I have loved you.' He is my Lord, my Boss. I must do as He says. Therefore, I love you. And all the other street boys I can reach."

"Oh, so you don't love me just because I'm such a nice guy."

"I wasn't a nice guy when Jesus loved me. Why should I expect you to be?"

"What you mean? Look at you! Good clothes shined shoes, you're real nice guy."

"But I wasn't always, Jaime. Where I came from wasn't quite as bad as Tondo, I admit, but it was a place with very little hope. It's called Appalachia. It's a country province, very poor. I went barefoot a good share of the time then. My father kicked me out of the house when I was sixteen. Said I was big enough to make my own way. Jaime, if it hadn't been for some good Christian people that loved me like Jesus said they should, and helped and encouraged me, I don't know where I would have wound up. That's why I want to help you. To pay them back their love."

"You say crazy things." Jaime laughed. Then his eyes narrowed. "Look, maybe out there in your world there is something called love. In the magazines they talk of love, in the movies they talk of love. But I tell you," he spat the words as the bitterness built up in him, "here, in the real world, love! Ha! I gotta get you first, before you get me. I fight. I hate. That's what's going to get me out of here! How you like that, Mr. Missionary!"

"Jaime, I don't. That's why I am offering you this time at the camp. I want you to learn of this love I am talking about. It's there. You just won't see it. But it's there."

"Ha!"

"You told me your family is no good. Your Papa's a drunk. Your Mama screams at you all the time and your sisters always tease you. And they are all stupid, right? OK then, why do you go home to them? Why do you bring them money?"

"Because —" Jaime looked down, trying to find the words. *How can I explain? What can I say,* he thought. *What can I say that makes sense and not sound stupid?* "Because—- they are my family. I can't just let them go — with Papa—"

"You mean you love them."

"No! Love is soft, just mush, no real thing. It has no strength. This — is different."

"You mean 'concern,' or maybe 'responsibility'?"

"Yeah. That's it. I gotta do it. But love — Ha!"

"OK. I'll be careful not to call it love. I don't want to get you mixed up."

Jaime looked at Art darkly. *You already got me mixed up,* he thought. *That stupid family. What do I feel for them? Why do I feel anything for them? It cannot be love.* Finally, aloud: "I think I go home now, Art. I don't want to talk anymore today."

"Sure thing, Jaime. Here, take the rest of the oranges. There is a paper about the camp in the bag. See you in a couple of days."

"Yeah, thanks. Hey, if I go to your camp, can I bring my friend Rio?"

"Why, sure. Be careful with Rio, Jaime. Be careful not to show him any love."

Jaime flashed into anger. "Shut up!" he screamed between clenched teeth. He turned and ran from Art as fast as he could.

3

"What you think, Rio? This camp Art told about look pretty good — with all that food and stuff, and it don't cost us nothin'."

Jaime and Rio were sitting on the curb of Sande Boulevard just north of the San Nicolas District. It was a place of shops and small factories. They had cruised the downtown area of San Nicolas with its large office buildings and stores. It was fun to look in the store windows at the merchandise and to walk with the well-dressed people. However, the trip had not been very profitable. They started into one store with the idea of doing a little shoplifting, but after one look at their appearance the guard chased them out before they got close to the first counter. The man at the magazine store let them read for about ten minutes, but when he saw they were not going to buy, he too chased them out. The number of opportunities to steal seemed to abound, but so did the number of guards. So, they came to the north part of the city. It was not so rich, but it was a lot safer.

The traffic in the streets included wagons, motor bikes, cars, light trucks, and the ever-present jeepney. Jeepneys were mini buses that had evolved from customized World War II jeeps. Except for the shape of the hoods, their origin would never be recognized. The bodies were bigger, seats had been added, and they were painted with the wildest designs in the most outlandish colors. Each owner lavished much care and attention on his beloved vehicle, decorating it with all manner of colorful and unusual objects, trying to make his the brightest, gayest, happiest jeepney in all Manila. The Filipinos loved color and they loved fiestas, and nowhere did that love express itself more vividly than in the jeepney. Those rolling fiestas, however, were a vital part of the public transportation of the city. There were hundreds of them running around, each driver picking the route he thought the most profitable.

"What do I think about that camp? I think it's a trap. Look, we robbed the guy. The only reason he want us to go to this 'camp' is to get us in jail or the army. Yeah! The army. That's it." Rio had things all settled in his mind.

"No, I don't think so. I think he tell the truth."

"Why should he?"

"Because he's a religious type. All those religious guys do crazy things like this. Look at this paper he gave me. See, Action International Ministries put on the camps. These religious guys don't lie. They give us all that stuff because they — because — I don't know why, but they always doin' this sort of stuff."

"Sure, Jaime, sure. Remember when we went to that church where they say we can eat. They kicked us out."

"But because we try to steal the cross off the father. We

got more brains now. They givin' it away. Why shouldn't we take it?" Jaime glanced critically at Rio. *Why do I bother with him?* he thought. *It's not love, that's for sure. Not that dumb-dumb. I guess I just want someone around I know. I should go without him. Then I would get all I want and not have so much trouble.*

Suddenly he spotted a target. "Hey! Look on that jeepney!" He pointed to the street. "You make like you're hit and I grab the bag. Let's go!"

The brightly painted jeepney was picking its way down the street, overloaded with passengers. A woman sitting in the front seat had a shopping bag hanging out from her arm. Rio was to run up to the front fender, slap it, and pretend he was hit. The driver would slow down, thinking he had had an accident, then Jaime would grab the bag from the woman, and they would both run. It was a good trick that almost always worked.

Rio started out with Jaime right behind him. The driver saw them and just honked his horn and shook his fist. Rio slapped the fender, and the driver yelled at him and never slowed at all. Jaime reached for the bag, but it was coming too fast. It gave him a good blow to the head, split, and dumped its contents all over the road.

The woman screamed, the driver yelled, Rio cursed, and Jaime just sat there and moaned. He rolled over in some broken eggs, slipped on a not-so-fresh fish, grabbed a couple of mangos, and ran.

In an alley a few blocks away they ate the mangos and dejectedly thought out their mistakes. Rio finally broke the silence.

"My friend, you're a mess. You all sloppy with egg and you stink like fish. I think that was a bag of garbage she had."

"It sure was when we got through with it." Jaime could not help laughing a little. "We mess that up more ways than one, didn't we? Let's go to the docks. I can go for a swim and maybe we can steal something big."

The waterfront was not far away. There they joined some other boys swimming near an old dock that was half wrecked and had been abandoned for years.

"Hey, look! You can see the water," Rio joked. "There is hardly any garbage in it at all!"

"Yeah. You can jump in and not hurt yourself. How high you gonna jump?" one of the boys challenged.

The dock itself was in ruins, but most of the pilings were still there. The cross-braces between them offered diving platforms, and the highest of all were the crumbling planks that had once formed the deck. They could be reached by careful climbing. Jaime looked at the boys and at the deck.

"I don'o," he said.

But he did know. With the challenge from the boys and the planks just *being there,* he knew he would have to jump from the highest part. He did not want to, but he would have to. "Let me swim first, Then I try it."

He ran down the bank and plunged in, clothes and all. He wore only a T-shirt and shorts, and they needed washing anyway.

They splashed and played in the water for a while, all being good swimmers, but soon they started the silent challenge of jumping off higher and higher places on the piles. As they jumped each yelled and whooped to draw attention to the height of his dive. Finally there were only the deck planks left to jump from.

"Hiiii!" Rio was the first one off.

"Hoooo!" One of the other boys dared to jump. The third chickened out.

Jaime slowly climbed the piles to the planks. Only one way could he prove himself better. That was to dive headfirst. Fear gripped his stomach as he looked down, way down, to the water. The others watched silently.

I gotta do it. I'm better than they are. I'm better. I'm tougher and better. He braced himself with ego thoughts. Then sucking in his breath, he launched himself headfirst off the deck. Fear tightened his stomach and his yell became a grunt. The water slammed his head, making him see stars, and his legs flipped over and smacked the water with a searing sting. Down and down he went until his hands slid into the mucky bottom. He panicked at the thought of getting caught in something, and clawed his way to the surface. It seemed to take forever. The feeling of suffocation was overwhelming by the time he broke water and gulped great sobbing lung-fuls of air.

I did it! I did it! he exulted to himself, happy that the water masked the tears of pain and panic. The others were wide-eyed in awe and admiration. No one made a move toward the piles to duplicate his feat.

With common assent they all climbed out of the water and sat on the bank to dry.

"Didn't that hurt?" The youngest boy, the one that had chickened out, asked.

"Oh, a little," Jaime admitted, showing how well he could bear pain. "Mostly the top of my head."

"Yeah! Wow!" Jaime basked in their admiration. It had been worth it after all.

After they dried, their attention was drawn to the docks with their piles of goods and bales of merchandise. There was more in the long warehouses. They searched for an opening in the chain link fence. Twice the guard yelled at them, making a big show of chasing them away. But Jaime saw a jitney, or forklift, driver purposely drive his machine into a box to break it open. The guard conveniently turned his back as the porters stripped the box of its contents.

That's for me, thought Jaime. *I can get a big gang here on the docks. I'll have trucks and jeepneys and men to drive them. They can steal and load the trucks and bribe the guards —* His mind wandered as he walked through the area.

"Hey, Jaime, c'mon. Let's go. We can't get nothin' here."

"No! Not yet. Let's look some more."

They slowly walked along. There were the small inter-island boats. Men, by hand, sweated out the cargos of food and copra and local produce. *Not much profit there,* Jaime thought. *But on the other hand, maybe if I got some stores—*

Next were the larger tramp freighters. Here, winches and booms replaced hands and sweat. Two booms worked together. Each boom had its own winch. A line from the winch ran out to the end, over a pulley, and was joined to the line from the other boom at a big hook. One of the booms was positioned right over the hatch in the deck being unloaded. The other boom of the pair was swung out over the side of the ship by the dock. Each boom was held in place with lines so it would not swing.

Somewhere in the hold the cargo was piled onto big cargo nets, and the four corners of the net, drawn together, were hooked onto the big hook. With a shout and a yell, the first winch operator would start to lift the load straight up out of the hold. Once it got clear of the deck, the second operator would start to pull tighter on his line, and the load would swing toward the dock. The first man would then slack off a little with his line, and if they both did it right, the load would move smoothly over the deck until it was hanging directly under the second boom, which took all the weight. The second operator would lower it down, more or less gently, onto the dock. The porters unhooked the load, hooked on an empty net, and, after that was lifted away, scramble over the loaded net carrying away the goods as directed by the boss.

Jaime watched and watched, unmindful of Rio's whining to go back. *There has to be a flaw in this,* he thought, *some way to steal.* If he was ever going to lead a gang here he had to study the ways that cargo was handled. He saw several boxes dropped and split open. No matter what the content, it immediately disappeared. *How did the porters get it out?* he wondered. Papa was somewhere down on the docks. He never brought anything home, so he must hock it.

Jaime watched the pattern. The swing of the cargo—up out of the hold, across the deck, down on the dock. The empties back the other way. Stark scare-crows, long and thin, going into the hold. Fat gluttons, heavy with wealth, coming out. He watched the men scramble over the piles on the nets. They loaded the boxes and bales on handcarts and wheeled them through various doors in the warehouse. Jitneys handled the bigger items. Sometimes a whole bunch of boxes were loaded on pallets and the forklift took them away.

From his vantage point outside the fence, Jaime could get an overall look at the pattern of movement. He noticed that every once in a while one of the porters, instead of going into the warehouse, would wheel his load all the way to the end of the building and load it into a small truck. His load was small, as if he was careful of what he took.

When the truck was full, the porter talked to the boss for a minute. Then he parked his handcart and climbed into the truck. The boss sent one of the other men over to the guard shack where he talked to the guard. Jaime could not hear what he said but noticed a lot of hand-waving and shouting. The man kept beckoning the guard away from the gate, pointing to a pile of boxes nearby. Finally the guard went over and looked at the pile. Just as he did so, the truck drove out the open gate. The guard ran back to stop the truck, but when he saw it was too late he yelled at the man who called him and grabbed him as if to turn him in. The boss and two other porters walked over to the struggling men. They were armed with the deadly cargo hooks used to handle bales and bundles. When the guard saw them coming, he stood for a minute, let the man go, shrugged his shoulders, and walked back to the gate. The men returned to their work.

Jaime's dream of leading a gang on the docks slowly crumpled into ashes at his feet. There *was* a gang on the docks. They were *already* raiding the cargo. And they were powerful enough to get away with driving a truck out the gate whenever they wanted to. The intimidation of the guard showed Jaime the strength they had. He had enough savvy in the ways of crime to know there was no way he, young punk that he was, would ever be able to break into that mob. If he tried to start another one, there would be nothing but gang warfare. That did not appeal to him at all. Stealing and taking the chances of getting caught were one thing, but violence and taking the chance of getting killed were something else again.

"C'mon, Jaime, we not gettin' anything here. Let's go!" Rio's complaint broke his thoughts.

Jaime looked at Rio. *I wonder,* he thought, *if I could get others to do the fighting for me. As leader I wouldn't have to. But how could I do it? I sure couldn't get Rio to fight for me. I have to show him everything to do. But if I get someone that's smart enough to lead the fight, then he's smart enough to lead the whole gang. And there I am — out.*

The blankness of the future momentarily overcame him. It looked as if there was not much hope. Just petty thievery and a bare living until he died or got caught. *It's not worth it. It's just not worth living this way. Maybe Rio and others don't mind, but I do.* The depression lasted only a short time. Soon his ambition and determination came back, and his spirits rose.

"You're right, Rio, nothin' here. Let's go." He got back on his feet and started down the road. "There must be somethin' somewhere along here we can pick up. Let's check the alleys back of those buildings."

They walked past the many small industries and factories located across the road from the docks. They searched the alleys behind them, looking for anything of value. There were others doing the same thing, and much of the junk was well picked over. Jaime found a board he thought he could use, and Rio had a couple of cartons under his arm, when a door opened right in front of them and a man came out with a large barrel and dumped it into the trash can. The tinkle of metal and glass drew their attention. They swooped down on it almost before the man was out of the way.

"Good hunting!" He smiled wryly at them as he watched them pick through the garbage to get at the cans and bottles. The metal and glass they could sell to a junk man for a few centavos, or maybe for even a peso or two, depending on the quality and quantity of the items. Other boys in the area heard the trash hit the can, and they came running. By the time they got there Jaime and Rio had all the best items and were on their way. Jaime dropped the board and was carrying one of Rio's cartons, now full of tin cans, bottles, and a few rags.

"Hey, that's pretty good haul. I bet we get four pesos fifty for this stuff." Rio was elated.

"Could be, if we talk Old Man Asin nice-like."

"You can talk good to him. I bet he gives us even more."

"Yeah, sure." Jaime's depression had not completely left him and the trash picking had just underlined the hopeless position of a street boy like himself. *There gotta be more to life than just this. Art has more to his life. But he said he came from a place like Tondo. Somehow or another he got out of his "Tondo." The only way I am ever going to learn anything from him is to go to the camp and see just what these people have. I gotta take the chance that it might be a trap or something. I gotta learn how these people got out.*

"Wait a minute!" Jaime put down his box to rest. "Ernesto, Little Mouse, came back."

"What you talking about? That dive hit your head too hard?"

"It's no trap. Don't you see? If it was a trap Ernesto would not come back. He would be in the army! I'm dumb not to think of that."

"You're dumb not to tell me what you are talking about!"

"The camp! The camp. Don't you see? Ernesto was at the camp and he came back. And all the other guys on that bus. They all came back."

"Yeah, that's right. But how many went? Maybe they only keep those they want."

"No, Ernesto would have said so. He don't lie to me. He's afraid of me. He wouldn't dare. You know that. He said they give you all kinda things. Like food. Hey, Rio, how you like to have your belly full each day? Ha! That sounds good."

"Yeah. What else he tell you they do?"

"Not much, but this paper tells more. Oh, no!" He pulled a soggy mess out of his pocket. The swim had done the paper no good. "I forgot!" He carefully peeled the folds apart and spread it out on his box to dry. "I remember what it said. There," he pointed to one section, "It said to bring toothbrush, towel, blanket, change of clothes, and somethin' else we don't have either." They looked at each other and smiled. "We can come anyhow even if we don't have all that stuff."

"That's good. I don't even know where to steal all that stuff, even if I had time to. Maybe I can bring my basketball?"

"That picture there shows guys playing basketball on a full-size place."

"Oh, boy! That's for me! I never played on full-size court. What else they show?"

"That's of guys playing softball. You ever play that? I haven't."

"Naw. It's like baseball. Maybe they show us how."

"Also it say we gotta study stuff. That's OK. Maybe we learn somethin' that helps us get more money." *Or helps me get out of here,* he added silently. It looked as if Rio was coming around, and he did not want to spoil anything.

"You think it's religious stuff?"

"If it is we don't have to listen. Just pretend —and eat and play basketball."

"Ah — Why not? When we leave?"

"Next Monday, I think." He carefully turned the drying paper over and looked at the date. "I guess that's next Monday. I find out from Art when I see him again. We better get going with this stuff if we want to get paid today." He carefully folded the paper again and put it back in his pocket. As he hoisted his box to his shoulder and started out, he thought: *Rio, my fren, I am going to that camp. I like to have you come with me. But I am going. Something, I don't know what, but something tells me that is where I am going to learn how to get out of Tondo.*

33

4

It was the day to leave for camp. Jaime woke early. The excitement of a new adventure drove sleep from him. He lay in his lean-to and smiled to himself. *Tonight I will know if it's the army or a new way of life. Ha! It's going to be a new way of life either way. The army sure will be different.* He started to laugh —then checked himself. He must be quiet and not wake the rest of the family. They might stop him or at least question where he was going so early, and he did not want to take any chances. He had not told them he was going, of course. They would have said no and raised all kinds of trouble.

He checked his hiding place and saw that the wallet and his magazines were all there. He carefully covered it and made sure no evidence was showing. He had sneaked his other shirt out of the house and rolled it into a package he could sling over his shoulder. That was the only thing on the list he had. He had never had a toothbrush and wondered what it was like to brush your teeth. The ads always made it seem like fun; at least the people were always smiling.

He listened carefully, but the only noises from the shack were Papa's snoring and Mama's loud breathing. He did not breathe easily until he was a block away. Then he straightened up and strode on his way through the early dawn to Rio's box.

Rio reluctantly opened his eyes. "Wasa matter? Who you? Oh, Jaime. It's hardly light! What you come now for? Go sleep, an' wake me in a coupla hours." He scrunched into a more comfortable position, pulled the newspapers up over himself, and started to go back to sleep.

Jaime laughed. "Come on, my fren, how can you sleep now? Just think; today! All we can eat and basketball on a big court. And you lay there like a sick dog. Come on, get up."

"What you so excited about?" Rio rolled over into a sitting position, yawned, and scratched himself. "You act like you never go to army camp before."

"Oh, Rio. You met Art. You met Mr. Lito. They told you all about the camp. Those religious guys don't lie."

"I don't trust Art. We robbed him. He's gonna get us. What else would he do? That Mr. Lito though, he's something else again."

He sure is, Jaime thought, *Mr. Lito Francisco has what I want. He said he was once a street boy himself. But now look at him: nice shirt, good pants, shoes, Director of Camp Ilaw — Camp Light— respected, a real leader. But there was more than that. There was an attitude, a feeling, he was so sure of himself so confident in what he did. That's what I call getting out! And that's what I want.*

Jaime and Rio had met Mr. Lito when they went over to ACTION Headquarters in San Juan to sign up for the camp. Art took them over there to meet some of the staff and to stop their fears about the army. It was a very nice place with all sorts of people going in and out. They all seemed to be happy, busy people, and there was no sign of the army anywhere. There were signs of Jesus, however. Jaime noticed the fish sign, like the one on the wallet, hanging on the wall. There were other posters and pictures around and all had Jesus on them.

Mr. Lito even bought them some *adobo* chicken for lunch at a little food stand down the street from the Action International Ministries building and told them about the camp and himself. He talked about his former life as a street boy and how he, too, had been helped out of it by good Christian people. Both the boys had been impressed; Rio by the stories of food and basketball, and Jaime by the evidence of the "good life" that all those people had. Obviously they had money. They had shoes, houses, they were clean, and above all, they were happy. What else could do that but money? That was what Jaime wanted.

They assured Art they could find their way back by themselves and he did not have to take them. Besides, they wanted to stop by the Frisco Market and see what they could steal. Art would have cramped their style.

That time they had a little better luck than the previous time. They got half a dozen loaves of *pandesal* bread, Rio took a tin cup out of an open shopping bag, and Jaime made off with four eggs. It was a good time for them. Mama liked bread and eggs as much as money, and would welcome Jaime home. Rio had fun showing off how he would drink out of his cup and use it to wash off his basketball.

"Why you come so early?" Rio dug the sleep out of his eyes. "We only have to go over to the school to get the bus at nine o'clock."

"I had to get away before Mama wake up or she would be on my back to do something."

"Hey, what you say we go over to the Quinta Market and get some breakfast?"

"I don't know, Rio. I don't want to take any chances today. If we get caught it louse everything all up."

"So what's different? Any time we get caught it louse things all up."

"But not today. Just think, we go on a long bus trip. You ever been on a bus before?" Jaime tried to divert Rio's thoughts.

"Nope! And that's what gives me a big appetite. We don't go to the market — I don't go."

What's getting into this guy? Jaime thought. *That's not like him. I bet he's still scared of the army and is looking for a way to back out.*

"OK. Let's go then. But you be careful. I don't want to spend a month in jail rather than a week at camp."

"Good!" Rio stood up, put his basketball under his arm,

and hooked his tin cup on the waistband of his pants. "Now I got everything. Let's go. I cannot think of a better way to start our new army career than breakfast of a couple of nice tasty mangos from Old Lady Columna's fruit stand."

Even that early the market was in full swing. The din was as loud as ever with the merchants hawking their wares and the customers haggling over the prices. They made their way through the bakery section and over to the fruit stalls and had not seen a chance to steal anything. It was starting to get late, and Jaime was getting more and more anxious.

"Come on, Rio! They feed us when we get there. Let's not waste time here."

"No. We get somethin' here." It was a new Rio, Jaime could not control him the way he used to.

"There! Old Lady is busy with customer. Hold this. I go." Rio thrust the basketball at Jaime and headed for the stand. He deftly picked two mangos off the rack and turned right into the arms of Old Man Columna.

"Ha! My thief, I got you this time. You no longer steal from us. I see to that. Guard! Guard!"

Jaime watched the scene with sinking feelings and tightening stomach. *The dumb-dumb. I try to tell him. What can I do? I cannot save him but I cannot leave him. I can't do anything. If I try then we both get caught. Oh, you dumb, dumb, dumb-dumb.* Rio cast a desperate glance at him as Jaime turned to go. *Goodbye, my stupid friend, if there is a next time, listen to one who is smarter than you.*

As Jaime turned he felt the basketball under his arm. Wait! He looked back at the scene. There was no guard yet. There was only Mr. Columna holding Rio, and Mrs. Columna was still busy with the customer. He ran back a few steps to get a good start, then started trotting toward the stand dribbling the basketball in front of him, whistling as he came. No one paid any attention to him. When he got to the stand he pretended to slip, hit the ball right at Mr. Columna's face, and bumped against the fruit table, making it tip. Mr. Columna yelled even louder, let go of Rio, and grabbed for the table.

"I'm sorry! I'm sorry! I slipped!" Jaime yelled to add to the confusion. He grabbed the ball and ran off. He never looked for Rio. If Rio could not get out of that by himself, there was not anything more Jaime could do.

When he broke out of the market into the street he found Rio right behind him.

Jaime shoved the ball back at him. "We go to the bus right now! No more fooling around or I bash your head in!"

"Wait a minute! I lost my cup. I want it back!"

Jaime drew back his fist but then stopped. *What good would it do,* he thought. *He is just stupid.* "No, my friend, we don't go back. We go on without it."

"But I want it."

Jaime smiled patiently as if Rio were a small boy. "Maybe we can get another one when we get back." Suddenly Art's words echoed in his mind, "Be careful with Rio, Jaime. Be careful not to show him any love."

But this is not love, he told himself. *This is wanting a friend along with me. What's wrong with that? I rescued him because I wanted — because — I didn't want to see him in jail. I'm not the kind of fellow that goes around loving people. I got more sense than that — I just like him. But do I like him now when he don't want to get to the bus? All the time before he does as I say. He is different now. This is like the time we got lost when we try to go to Makati to see the new buildings. He act funny then, too. I bet he's just scared.*

"Hey, Rio, are you scared? Scared to go to camp because you think the army gonna get you?"

"No! I'm not scared of anything!"

"Then come on. It's getting late."

"I want somethin' to eat first."

Jaime's patience finally reached its limit. "Look, you dumb-dumb, if we don't hurry the bus will be gone!"

"Who you calling a dumb-dumb!"

"I'm callin you a dumb-dumb, you dumb-dumb! We gonna miss that bus and it's gonna be your fault!"

"Don't you call me a dumb-dumb! You think you so hot! You go — take that bus and land in the army. But not me! See if you so smart! Ha!"

"I am smart! You'd be in jail now if I not smart to save you! You starve if I not teach you how to steal!"

"OK, smart guy! Go jump in the army! I don't care. I'm not going!"

"Well then good-bye, dumb-dumb! You see! I come back even smarter. And with a full belly, too! Go rot in jail. See if I care." Jaime turned toward the school where the bus was and trotted off.

"Hup, two, three, four. Hup, two, three, four." Rio started marching up and down like a soldier. Jaime ran faster until he was out of sight.

That Rio, he thought, *now is a fine time to let me down. Here was the chance to find our way out of this mess and you go chicken. Well, I'm not going to give up my chance for you or anybody. We can learn from these people. We have to learn. You will never let me down again, that's for sure. Even if you're not in jail when I get back, I'll still not have you for buddy anymore.*

But you will wind up in jail if I'm not there to keep you out. He slowed for a minute as a feeling of guilt overcame him. *No! Rio left me — I didn't leave him. I suppose all friends split up sooner or later. That's too bad. Rio was kinda dumb but he was a nice guy. I'm gonna miss him. But I'm not gonna miss that bus and a chance to get out of here. Not for Rio or anyone.*

He sighed in relief when he spied the big red bus still in front of the school. A Filipino man was checking the names. Art was nowhere in sight.

"Hi, there, fellow, what's your name?" The stranger had an easy grin.

"Jaime Jorka."

"OK, Jaime, pleased to meet you. My name's Ernie Cochon. Hop aboard. We're just about to leave. I have only one name left, Rio Rodriquez. You know him?"

"Yeah. I don't think he's comin'. He said he won't."

"That's too bad. We'll wait a while to see if he shows up. If not, you can tell him what fun it was and maybe he'll go next time."

Jaime had never been on a bus. He had hitched some rides on jeepneys and been in the back of a truck, but he had never been on a big bus like that. His nostrils flared at the strange smells inside the bus. The only seat was at the end of the long, narrow aisle and the ridges on the floor felt funny to his bare feet. The plastic seat was almost too hot from the sun to sit on, but he eased himself onto it, trying to act cool and relaxed, not letting on that it was all new to him.

Ernie came aboard, and Jaime jumped as the engine roared to life under him. Funny hissing and creaking noises came from inside the machine as it started out from the curb. Jaime's heart pounded as they started on their way. He looked out the window as the school slid by, and there was Rio, the basketball under one arm, a stick over one shoulder like a rifle, marching up and down. Jaime turned his head away with a snap. The shame of his defeat, the defeat of not getting Rio to go with him, washed over him.

5

Jaime had seen pictures of the countryside, but this was the first time he had been out in it. The bus joined several others at Caloocan City, and they proceeded in caravan fashion around the north of Manila Bay to the Bataan Peninsula where the camp was located. In school he remembered pictures of rice paddies and the oxenlike carabao pulling plows, but now he was actually seeing them!

The boys had been rather quiet when the bus first started, but they were all as excited as Jaime at the new sights. Ernie and the other counselors that had joined him in Caloocan City were busy going up and down the aisles answering the boys' questions and getting to know them.

"Sure, that's a banana tree." Ernie was talking to a boy in the seat ahead of Jaime. "You've seen them before in Manila, haven't you? They're a little bigger out here, but the same thing." He swung back to Jaime's seat. "And what do you think of all this, young fella?" His smile was infectious.

"I never seen a rice field before." Jaime could not help but smile back. "Do those farmers get lots to eat? They should with all that food they grow."

"That's a pretty deep question, er — Jaime." Ernie looked

at his name tag. "They get enough, but they're raising that food to sell, not to eat. And it costs them something to do it, seed, feed for the carabao, rent for the land, things like that. They don't get rich doing it, that's for sure. Why you ask? You want to be a farmer?"

Jaime laughed at the question. "I don't know anything about it. I was just wondering. What do you do, Ernie? I don't think you make a living at camp. Or do you?" The thought intrigued him.

"You're pretty sharp, and you're right. I do this for fun. I'm a Bible student — studying to be a pastor of a church, or a missionary or something."

"Does that pay pretty good?"

"Oh, my, no. Not in money, anyhow."

"Then why you do it?"

"Jaime, you ask me that question again, at the end of the camp. You'll understand better then. OK?"

"Meanwhile, look at the scenery and smell the fresh air." Ernie threw his head back and sniffed loud and long. Everybody around him laughed.

"Hey, Ernie, where is this place? When we gonna get there?" someone asked.

"We'll be there in about an hour. It's Camp Ilaw — Camp Light — and it is on the shore of Manila Bay on Bataan. You all remember Bataan and the Death March, don't you?" There was a mixed chorus of yeses and nos. "What! Some of you don't know about our most shining hour? When forty-seven thousand Filipinos and three thousand Americans held out for three months against an invading force of three hundred thousand Japanese? For shame! It was the noblest defeat in the whole of World War Two."

As he went on to tell of the final fall of Corregidor and of the brutal Death March of the defenders 150 miles of the peninsula to Camp O'Donnel, Jaime remembered the day he first heard of it in school. That same feeling came back to him again — a mixture of fear and shame. He knew that he, Jaime Jorka, would not have had the guts to go through a thing like that.

He shook his head as he pulled himself out of his reverie and looked at the scenery flashing by. The *nipa* huts of the farmers, made entirely of thatch and set up on stilts, looked pretty good to a Tondo boy. They sure were a lot nicer than the hovels most of his friends lived in.

There were fewer and fewer farms, and the jungle became thicker and thicker the farther they traveled from Manila.

"How you like to be lost in that?" his seatmate asked, pointing to the dense foliage.

"Well, at least you wouldn't have to worry about getting hit by a jeepney." They both laughed.

"Or have the police find you."

"It would take the whole army to find you if you really got very far into it."

"That's right, Jaime." Ernie joined them. "During the war, bands of guerrilla fighters — the underground army they called them — lived and fought in this jungle. The enemy never could find them. All they could do was secure towns. They never controlled the jungle. They'd send out patrols that were never heard from again. Even today it's not too safe. They say there are bandit gangs and outlaws living back there."

"Is there anything you don't know about this place?" Jaime gently kidded Ernie.

"Not much." He laughed. "I've been here several times and I also read up on it."

That's smart, thought Jaime, *but every time I go into a bookstore they chase me out because they know I'm gonna steal something. Maybe I find out from Ernie how to read that stuff without having to steal it.*

Suddenly the bus slowed down. The strange hissings and groans from underneath sent a chill of fear through Jaime. Was something wrong? Had the bus broken down? Everyone was tense and silent, waiting to see what would happen.

"We're almost there!" Ernie shouted as the bus turned off the main road onto a narrow dirt one. The dust swirled up into the bus, but it had the smell of clean, outdoor dust and not the stench of Tondo dust. A cheer went up when they came into a large clearing on the shore of the bay. They had arrived at camp.

"OK, now, everybody off the bus and over to the meeting area. Right over there where that man is standing. C'mon now, let's go. Don't go anyplace else; go right to the meeting area." Ernie and the other counselors herded the boys over to the area.

Jaime looked around as they waited for the others to arrive. One of the first things that caught his eye was the full-sized basketball court. He quickly brushed Rio out of his mind and continued to get the lay of the land. The buses had parked behind a big shed like building. He could not see into it, but he noticed an outdoor kitchen at one end with its big pots and open fires. Next to that was a long, low building with several doors in it. There was at least one person standing in each doorway watching them arrive.

Off, away from the beach, through the palm trees he could see a series of smaller buildings like the *nipa* huts of the farmers, except those were made of plywood. The campground was mostly level, grass with palm trees, but it also had a large open field and backstop for softball or soccer. Several more buildings he could not quite see were behind the big shed. The smell of the salt water was sweet to his nose. He cocked his head and listened. Over the sound of the waves and the rustle of the trees he caught the sound of sawing wood and the beat of a hammer. *Oh, boy, they just finish it in time for us to get here,* he thought.

At the meeting area, rows of benches were set in a half circle on a slight slope of ground. Mr. Lito stood in the front talking to some men. Jaime's heart gave a leap as he recognized Art standing with the others. Someone called down that they were all there, and Mr. Lito walked over to a little stand and held his hands up for silence.

The boys quieted down quickly, intent on hearing what was really going to happen.

"I want to welcome you all to Camp Ilaw. It's good that all of you came. I know some of you don't understand what's happening, but this is a Christian camp, a Bible camp, and you will have one of the greatest times you ever had in your life.

"But we have rules. There aren't too many of them, but we do have them. If you break those rules and give us any trouble, we will ship you back to Manila. You understand? OK. Now here are the basic rules: One. You will each be assigned to a cabin, with a counselor. You will stick with that group in all your activities. Two. There will be no leaving the campgrounds. Three. Your counselor is boss. Listen to him. And four. Above all, no fighting.

"We got things for you to do all day long. Your counselor knows what they are and will lead you to the activities. We have sports like basketball, swimming, softball, and stuff. Handcrafts like kite building and flying. We'll have lots of Bible study. And you will even have some free time to do as you want, like siesta!

"Now one thing I *know* you won't want to do is eat, so I won't tell you about that." There were a few calls from the crowd. "What?! You *do* want to eat?" More calls as the boys caught on to the joke. "You mean you want to eat *food?*" A giant yell. "Why should we feed you? All you'll want to do is eat again." Mr. Lito took a small sponge ball out of his pocket. "If we feed you it will be just like this ball." He stuffed it into his closed left hand. "And like this," he pulled another one out and did the same. "And like this." A third one. "You will stuff all that food into your mouth and then in a little while it will be all gone, and you will want to eat again." He slowly opened his hand. All the balls had disappeared. A moment of stunned silence, then wild shouts of laughter.

Jaime sat unmoving, watching Mr. Lito, amazed at the skill of the man. *He is fooling us, almost as I fool Rio,* he thought, *but he is not cheating us. He is just being funny. Then we will all trust him. He is smart; very, very smart.*

"All right, all right. If you want to eat, I tell you what we will do. Whenever you hear a real loud bell, and I mean a *real loud* one, you all go over to that big building right there, on that side, and line up, and go inside and eat."

A loud electric bell started ringing. "That's it! Take your bundles with you and line up like I told you! Let's go! Eat!"

Pandemonium broke out as all the boys leaped up and tried to be first. The counselors were already at the doors lining up the boys to go in. Jaime was near the front and could hardly believe his eyes.

Tables and benches in long rows filled the whole hall. At

each place were plastic trays, red and green and yellow and blue, and cups of the same colors. Each tray was full of as much food as a whole family would eat at once. There was a big pile of rice in one compartment, another held spaghetti, another *paksiw* fish. *Pandesal* bread filled the last one. There were bowls of jam and pitchers of fruit juice on the table. The smell was delicious.

"Everybody wait! Stand in back of the bench until we are all inside and Lito says grace. Everybody wait!" The counselors tried to slow things down and maintain control.

Jaime did not pay any attention to the voices. His stomach talked louder. He found an empty place, leaped over the bench, and started to wolf down the food. It was the first he had eaten since yesterday noon.

"Jaime! Didn't you hear what they said?" Art's familiar voice got his attention. He hunched over his food in a protective gesture. Art reached his hand out to touch his shoulder, and Jaime pulled away in an almost reflex action. Suddenly he stopped. *I could be sent home!* he thought. He sat there stricken. Slowly he started up, loathe to leave the food. As he stepped back over the bench he heard a voice saying: "Thank you, Lord. Amen."

"It's too late now, Jaime. Go sit down." Art sat a few places away. Hardly a word was spoken as the boys set themselves to the task. Jaime ate more slowly now, looking around, wondering what was going to happen to him for his breach of rules. He expected any moment his tray would be taken and he would get no more to eat.

"Hey, you outa rice. You want some more?" A young fellow not much older than Jamie was behind him, his cart loaded with steaming rice.

"It's OK? You not mad at me?" Jaime looked at Art then at the server.

"Sure, sure. Eat all you want. That's what we are here for." Art's smile was full of love and forgiveness. "Just don't let it happen again."

Jaime grinned at the server. "Just a little more. Not too much. I'm getting full."

"Here you go." He plunked a big scoopful onto Jaime's plate. "If you want some more fish there is another guy right behind me with some of that."

The noise level slowly picked up as the boys finished eating. Jaime could not take a single swallow more. He tried to finish the last of his fruit juice and could not. For the first time he could ever remember, he was stuffed.

"Hey, look at that!" he pulled his shirt tightly over his belly. "That's the first time I see you stick out," he addressed his middle. "Many time I see you stick in, but never I see you stick out like that!"

"Me too!" his seatmate cried. "Yeah, look at that." Up and down the table the boys started to compare bellies. One younger fellow looked up with wide eyes.

"I think I'm gonna be sick!"

"No. No. Don't waste the food. Hold it down!"

"Keep it, keep it," the others yelled at him.

Art's eyes shone with laughter as he entered into the good-natured jokes and contented feeling of the boys around him.

"Attention, please. Attention, please." Mr. Lito was standing on a small platform at one end of the hall. "Now look, fellows, when we bring you in here to eat we expect you to *eat*. See," he held up his hands, "there is one teaspoon of rice and half a piece of *pandesal* left over. What's the matter? Don't you like our food? How come you're not eating everything?" Groans and laughs drowned out his voice. "OK, OK" he quieted them, "we forgive you this time. Just don't let it happen again."

"Now for the next hour or so there isn't much to do except find your cabin. I will call out a number — that will be the cabin number — then I will call out a bunch of names. Those will be the boys in that cabin. OK? Now keep the noise down so you can hear your name. If you don't hear your name, come see me at the end. The first cabin, number one. The counselor is holding up a sign with a number one — go to him—"

Jaime listened and waited for his name. Finally at cabin 8 he heard his name. He did not recognize any other names, so he figured the boys must be from some other district. He did notice, however, that it was Ernie Cochon who was holding the sign.

The cabin was about twenty feet long and almost as

wide. The floor was built several feet off the ground, as was the small porch at one end. The walls were solid to a height of about five feet, then just screened to the roof. The roof had a generous overhang to keep the rain out, and there were shutters that could be closed against typhoons. Three double bunks were on each side, a table and chairs in the middle, and a small room with two bunks at the far end.

Jaime tossed his bundle on a top end-bunk where he could look out at the bay.

"As soon as our other counselor get here with the hygiene kits we will start on that. Meanwhile just take it easy and try to digest that meal. That little back room is ours. This big room is yours. One thing we gotta do is keep this place clean. There is a prize for the cabin that is kept the cleanest. Each day they are inspected and anything out of place is marked down." Ernie rattled on about rules and schedules.

Jaime climbed up to his bunk and sat in it, leaning against the wall, and looked out over the camp. A warm contentment spread from his full belly over his whole body. It was so peaceful.

"OK, Jorka, on your feet! Snap it up there!" Jaime jerked awake to stare into Art's smiling face.

"Hey, please, Art, don't you scare me like that. I think I'm in the army, and you know how I feel about *that*."

"While you been sleeping, my friend, Ernie and I divided up the cabin. I get this half. He gets that. So, my poor boy, you got me for your counselor. Think you can stand it?"

"I don't know, but I try." Jaime had trouble not letting his happiness show. He jumped down from the bunk, and Art introduced him to the others.

"This is Luis, Rudy, Pat, Manual, and Poi. And this is Jaime. Now we all know each other. Let's go outside, over by where the sinks are." They tromped over to the line of spigots outside the latrines. Other groups gathered around their counselors, all getting the same instructions.

"This is a hygiene kit." Jaime recognized the cloth bag Little Mouse had carried off the bus. "In it is a cake of soap. Anybody know what it's for?"

"Don't rich people put it on bread and eat it?"

"No. You put it on things to make them slip."

"Girls wear it around their necks to make them smell pretty."

"Say, you guys are pretty smart. But I'll show you another thing you can do with it; it's called *washing*. We are going to do that before every meal. Like this—" Art had them all go through the motions of hand washing, hair combing, and finally, tooth brushing. Jaime ran his tongue over his strange-feeling teeth and tingling gums.

He liked the feeling, but did not think it good enough to smile as they did in the ads. "— This is called *grooming*. We will do it every day.

"The next thing is a clean you. Your clothes and your

body. Now one of the easiest ways to wash your clothes is to leave them on when you go swimming."

The bay was warm and clean, Art showed them how to tramp their clothes in the clean sand of the beach and then lay them out on the grass to dry. Jaime reveled in the clean water, He even rubbed some of the sand on himself. *If it's good for the shirts, it must be good for me,* he reasoned.

All too soon Art called them out. "If your clothes aren't dry yet, put them on anyhow. They'll dry on you as well as on the grass."

Jaime pulled his short trousers over his wet underwear but left his shirt off. The breeze on his bare skin felt good. He hung his shirt carefully on a bush outside the cabin where it could dry fully.

He noted lesson number one in his mind. Be clean. All the counselors and staff were clean. All the rich people were clean. It would be hard to do in Tondo, but Jaime vowed: *From now on, I will be clean.*

"We got about twenty minutes till the general meeting, so if you want to look the camp over, now is a good time to do it." Jaime took him up on it and started on a tour of the whole place.

He circled the mess hall and found where the inside kitchen was, where they stored the food, and all other such details. The long low building with all the doors was the headquarters building. The offices for the camp were there, and some of the staff lived there. Every place he went, and every door he looked into, he got a cheery greeting and a big hello. *Maybe that should be lesson number two. Be nice to people. I'll try it. See if it works. Be polite and be happy.*

He heard the banging of the hammer again and decided he had time to find where it was coming from. Behind the headquarters building were the garages and work sheds.

Two carpenters were building an addition to the storeroom. They had the floor in and were framing one of the walls. They had nailed the wall together on top of the floor and were getting ready to set it up into place.

Jaime thought of his lean-to and window and other things he had built. They were so rough and crude compared to the carpenters' work. Here the boards were cut clean and square, and all the corners fit, Even the sawdust smelled clean. He wondered how it would feel to be proud of something he had made because it was right, rather than feeling frustrated knowing that a mess was the best he could do with what he had.

What they were doing looked like fun. He wondered if they would let him help them. Remembering lesson number two, be nice, Jaime approached them and said politely, "May I help you, sir?"

The carpenter looked at him and smiled. "Why sure thing, son. We're about to lift this wall up, and we could use another set of hands right now. Come on up here and lift right there when I tell you. Then you two can hold it while I brace it." Jaime did as he was told and soon had the satisfaction of seeing one skeleton wall standing in place. He did not have much time to admire it though. His time was about up.

"I gotta go now. There is a meeting," he excused himself.

"Thanks for the help, son. Come back anytime. We can always put you to work." Jaime basked in the glow of their appreciation. *Maybe these things really work,* he thought. *Here I am clean and I talk nice to them and they don't chase me away but ask me to come back. Not bad. Not bad at all. And I only been here a coupla hours.*

When he got back to the cabin he found Luis in his bunk. *Remember lesson number two, be nice,* he thought.

"Luis, there must be some mistake. That is my bunk you are in. Get out, please."

"You right there's a mistake if you think I gonna get out. You got that bunk now." Luis pointed to a lower one.

"My fren, I said get out, please." Lesson number two, be nice, suddenly went out the window as Jaime jumped up, grabbed Luis by the arm and flipped him out of the bunk onto the floor. Jaime started to climb into it when Luis grabbed Jaime's feet and dragged him onto the floor. His arm got a mean scratch on the edge of the bunk rail as he went down. Both boys were street-wise fighters, and as Jaime tried to land on Luis, Luis twisted out of the way, putting Jaime off balance.

Art and Ernie came bounding out of their room and

pulled the two boys apart.

"Hold it! Stop! You know there is no fighting allowed!"

Jaime was quick to recover. "My fren Art, we were not fighting. I fell out of my bunk and unfortunately, by accident, happened to land on fren Luis. We were just untangling ourselves when you came out." It was the best he could do on such quick notice. He hoped it would keep him from being sent home.

Art and Ernie exchanged glances, both trying to suppress the twitch of a smile.

"I see. If that's the case, then, Jaime, you must apologize to Luis for the accident. Will you?"

"Yes." *Anything to stay here.* "I apologize, Luis, for falling on you." Luis accepted with a nod and a grin at Jaime's discomfort.

"Now, Jaime, put your stuff up on your bunk where it belongs, And, Luis, put your stuff down on yours." Luis's smile faded quickly. "Jaime, come with me." Art reached out for Jaime's shoulder, but he twisted away as usual. He just did not like anyone touching him.

"Where we goin'?" He was suddenly suspicious as they headed across the lawn.

"Over to the headquarters building."

Jaime's hope crumbled as he realized he was going to be sent home.

6

"In here." They had reached the headquarters building, and Art directed Jaime through a door.

"Hello, there." A young lady wearing white clothes and a funny white cap greeted them. "What can we do for you?"

"Check his arm, will you?"

"That doesn't look too bad." She smiled encouragingly. "My name is Evelyn Rivera; I'm the nurse here. What's your name?" Evelyn made conversation as she went about getting out a bottle and a piece of gauze.

"Jaime Jorka." He watched her preparations anxiously. This was all new to him.

"This will sting a little, but it'll kill any germs in that scratch." *It stings more than a little,* Jaime thought, as she swabbed the antiseptic on his wound. His pride kept him from flinching.

"That should take care of it, but if it gets all red and starts to swell up, you come back." Her hands were cool and gentle on his skin as she ministered to him. "While you are here we might as well give you your checkup." She got out a form, put his name at the top and started checking him over. She looked in his mouth, in his eyes, listened to his chest with a stethoscope, made him laugh when she looked in his ears and commented: "Can't see through!" and felt around his neck and jaws. She had such a soft touch and gentle hands!

Jaime would not have admitted it for the world, but by the time she was through he was completely smitten. He had never in his life met anything or anyone as lovely as nurse Evelyn Rivera. It was rather disturbing.

"We gotta hurry if we're gonna make the general meeting." Art brought him back to reality.

"You're not gonna send me home?" Jaime dared to hope again.

"Not this time," Art kidded. "Just be careful. Don't — er — fall on anyone again."

"I won't. I won't!" A big grin split his face. *These people are really different. They don't hold grudges at all. It seems that almost anything you do they forgive you. That may be lesson number three. Don't hold grudges.*

Or at least don't act like you hold grudges. Jaime's old suspicious nature came back in full force. *Don't let your guard down. Just because some nice lady treats you good is no reason to get all soft.*

They joined the rest of the boys in their group at the meeting place. Mr. Lito was just starting as they arrived.

"Starting today, things are going to be different for you. Why? Because you start studying this." He held a blue-and-white-covered book up for them all to see. "What is it? It's the Bible. This book can change your life so much you won't believe it."

You bet. That's right, Jaime thought. Suddenly he remembered those same words when Art told him about the camp. *I didn't believe that either. But look where I am now.*

"It can change your life like this." Lito held up a black silk handkerchief. He started to stuff it into his left hand. About halfway through he started to pull it out the other side of his hand. It was now white. He kept stuffing in the black and pulling out the white until it was all through. He then opened his hand to show there was nothing in it.

"Just like that. Your life can be changed. How do I know? Because my life was changed. I started out on the street just like you. I stole. I raided garbage cans. Peddled junk. All the things you have done, I did. But look at me now. I'm standing here and you sit there. I got nice shirt, nice shoes, nice pants. What's the difference?

"I got Jesus Christ. And you don't.

"Did Jesus Christ drive up in a big car and rain down money on me that I got this way?" Jaime winced again at his own words coming back to him. "No. I got Him in my heart. In my head. He lives inside of me and shows me the right things to do so I don't blow it. You can have Him, too, if you want Him. That's why we're giving you this Book."

There was a general hubbub as the Books were given out. Jaime wanted to keep the first one he got, but he had to pass it on to Pat and Luis who were sitting alongside him. He looked at his for a moment, fondling it, turning it around in his hands. It was the first book he ever owned. *So this is the Book that got them out of the slums,* he thought. *This is the one thing they all have: knowledge of this Book. This may be lesson number four. Learn all you can about this Book.*

"Let's take a look at this Book, for a minute." Mr. Lito's voice quieted the boys. "You can put your name on the Book. Right on the front, where everybody can see it." Jaime took the pencil that came with the notebook and wrote his name on the upper edge of the Bible and the notebook. He held them out and looked at them. *Maybe I should make them a little fancier,* he thought. *I should —* "Now let's open the Bibles to page one," Mr. Lito went on. He paused until the rustling stopped. "Notice it says: 'The Good News Written by Matthew, Chapter one.' Then every so often there is a little number in with the words —" He went on to explain about chapter and verse, and about all the different books within that one Book.

Finally he said: "Let's turn to the book of John, chapter three verse sixteen. Can you find it? As soon as you do, raise your hand." Jaime scrambled through the pages and shot up his hand when he got it. He looked around and noticed that although he was not the first, there were not many that had their hands up before his.

"Several of you have found it. What page is it on? — page two hundred?" He acknowledged several calls, Jaime's among them. "That's right. Let's read what it says. 'For God so loved the world that He gave His only Son. Whoever puts his trust in God's Son will not be lost, but will have life that lasts forever.' You all see that?"

"Read it again, to yourselves." Mr. Lito repeated it for those who could not read. "That's a pretty big promise, isn't it? It is so big that it is going to be the first thing we'll study. Write this in your notebooks, right on the first page: 'God loves me. John three: sixteen.' You got that? 'God loves me. John three: sixteen.'

"This is the end of the meeting. We'll break now and meet with your counselors and study with them. We'll close in prayer. When we pray, we bow our heads and close our eyes, and think of the words that are said, and think of Jesus. Let's pray.

"Heavenly Father, we thank You for sending us Your Son to take away our sins and to make us all right in Your eyes. We think it is wonderful that You loved us so much that You sent us Your Son to die in our place, that we might have life forever with Him. Send Your Spirit down on each one of these boys, that they will receive Him and be saved from Your anger. Lord, You did it for each of us, now I ask that You do it for each of these boys. Thank You, Jesus. Amen.

"You are dismissed."

Art led the boys over to a place behind the huts under a palm tree. They all flopped on the grass around Art. Jaime opened his Bible and started to read.

"Where're you from, Art?" Poi asked.

"From the United States. Why did you ask?"

"I thought that was your accent, but sometimes it is hard to tell from an Englishman."

"No. An Englishman always sounds different." Manual spoke up.

"Anyhow, why did you come here? Couldn't you find a job in the States?" All the boys snickered.

"No, not that." Art laughed. "It was to help set up camps like this. In the States we do a lot of this sort of thing. There are lots of Bible camps. I came here to help the Mission get organized and staff camps for kids like you."

"Ha! I don't believe it!" Jaime closed the Bible with a thump.

"Why, Jaime, what a thing to say. Why shouldn't you believe me?"

"I don't mean you. I mean what the Bible says. It says Jesus didn't have any father. No father at *all*. That's silly. Everybody has a father, even if you don't know who he is."

"You learned something strange about Him, didn't you? Where were you reading?"

"From the beginning. Where else?"

"Remember what Mr. Lito said about this being a bunch of smaller books collected together in one big Book? Well, we have to be a little careful where we read. What you read was a book written by a man named Matthew. It is the story of Jesus' life. It's strange, isn't it?"

"Ha! It's crazy!"

"No. Jesus is *God's* Son. How do we know that?"

"Because God is his Father!" Poi could not keep still.

"Right! You've been talking to one of our gospel teams, haven't you, Poi?"

"Yeah. Severino and Raymond."

"What else did you learn about Him?"

"We learned He died and then came back to life again."

"How do you know?!" Jaime interrupted. "Just because this Book says so? How we know it tells the truth? Other books lie."

"Jaime, how do you know the Japanese were here? Have you met any? Do you know anyone that was here in the Death March? It was all before you lived, wasn't it? But you believe it because you read about it in history books. And smart people have studied those books — like your teachers — and they tell you that it's true, that it's history, that it happened. Well, it's the same with this Book. It *is* history. Many, many, many smart people have studied this Book, have gone to the land where it happened, have dug up the ruins in the place, and have found out it was all true. And then there are people like myself and Mr. Lito and all the counselors who have done what the Book says to do, and we all found out that what it says is true.

"Now let's get on with the study."

Jaime picked up the Book with more respect. He turned it over in his hands a few times.

"If I want to read ahead where should I read?"

"Start with the book of Mark. On page seventy-three. If you have any questions, write them in your notebook and ask me when you get a chance.

"Now let's turn to that verse on page two hundred. 'For God so loved the world He gave His only Son.' That is Jesus. Who is He? Why is He? What is He? Jaime found out He didn't have a man for a father, and Poi found out He came back from the dead. Now there is a lot of ground to cover between those two points. So, now open your Bibles to—"

Jaime tried to keep his determination not to study this "religious" stuff, but he became more and more fascinated with the story of a person that lived almost two thousand years ago. The things He did, like feeding five thousand people, and the things He taught, like loving even your enemies, were amazing. He certainly was different than anyone else that Jaime had ever heard about.

But it is just a story. No one could really be like that. At least I haven't seen anyone like that, he told himself. *But what about Art? and Mr. Lito? and the other counselors? Don't they show love like Jesus said you should? Yes, but I can't do it. Why not? Showing love and feeling love are two different things. That must be it! They just show love. It is a way to get people—*

"What's that!?"

"The dinner bell!"

"Again? We ate once already today!"

"And we eat again. On your feet, fellows. Hurry your books over to the hut and wash your hands real quick. We'll all line up and go in to eat together. *Move it!*"

In utter disbelief the boys filed into the mess hall and looked at the food piled on the trays. Rice and *adobo* pork and vegetables and *pandesal* and fruit and juice — twice in one day!

For this, thought Jaime, *I will do anything.* He stood respectfully behind the bench while Mr. Lito asked God to bless the food. That time he did not wolf down the food, but savored every bite. A hushed and reverent attitude fell over all the boys as they quietly spoke to each other, as if they were afraid it was a dream and they would all wake up back in Manila.

Jaime watched the counselors as they ate. He tried to duplicate their motions. The way they held their forks and spoons. The way they ate and drank. He used every opportunity to learn from those people. He tried using "please" and "thank you" as he asked for more juice or another loaf of *pandesal.* Art quietly encouraged the other boys to do the same, and soon they were the most polite bunch of street urchins anyone ever wanted to see. *Boy, oh, boy,* thought Jaime, *we will do anything and be anything just to get a full belly. And why not? What else is life about except a full belly? Once that is full then I will think of other things. That is why I want to get to be something. So I can fill my belly.*

"You guys are doing pretty well," Art commented. "I

wonder how long all this politeness will last? What do you think, Ernie?"

"Why, Art, it will last forever. They have now learned the good way and they will always do it. Won't you, boys?"

"Oh, sure! Absolutely! Always!" The boys chorused agreement.

"That's right," Jaime added, "but just gimme da bread or I'll hit ya." A roar of laughter greeted his remark. He was pleased at his own cleverness.

After supper they sat around under the trees waiting for the evening meeting. The boys grouped around Art asking him one question after another. He quietly and patiently answered all that he could. He joked and laughed and asked them things in return. He never belittled or scolded them, no matter how silly they became. Jaime listened for a while. Then he started to read the gospel of Mark. The story gripped him as he read of the Man and His ministry of healing the sick and the lame and the blind. In his imagination he walked with Him on the dusty roads of ancient Israel; and the sick and the lame and the blind of Tondo went with him.

"God loves you." Mr. Lito was the speaker at the night meeting.

He sure does, thought Jaime. *That's why he had me born in Tondo.*

"You may not think so. You say; if He loves me why was I born a poor street boy?"

The hair on Jaime's neck started to crawl. *Does he know every word I think?* There was a general rustle in the crowd as other boys looked around with big eyes. *No,* thought Jaime, *he just knows us well, can guess what we think. He is very smart.*

"You learned a lot about Jesus today. You learned many strange things about His life, His death, and His love for all people. Remember how He helped and healed all that came to Him? Not just his friends, not just those who had money, but everybody that came to him. OK, now, why don't *you* know this love? How come *you* never saw any of the good things that we say God the Father has for you?" Mr. Lito went on, giving example after example from the Bible of God's love for mankind. But each time he would come back to that same question: "Why doesn't God the Father show you some?"

God the Father, Jaime thought. *God the Father sure is different from my father. God loves us, but we don't see any love. So what. Does my father love me? I don't see any of his love. My father's too wrapped up in his drinking. He's so drunk he maybe don't even see me.*

On the other hand maybe he does see us. His son a thief. His wife a screaming nag. His daughters headed the same way. What would happen if he did show us any love? I'd pick his pocket when he hugged me, Mama would nag him about being up to something, and his daughters would just laugh at him. No wonder he drinks. There isn't much else he can do —

"All right, I've shown you that God does love you." Jaime's attention was back on Mr. Lito. "And now I'll tell you why you don't see any of it."

"First let me ask, do you deserve it? Are you so great that an infinite God, so powerful that He made the whole world, should love you?

"He said: 'Don't steal.' Is there anyone here that has never ever stolen anything?

"He said: 'Don't lie.' Is there anyone here that has never ever told even the smallest lie?

"He said: 'Honor your mother and father.' Is there anyone here that has never ever been mad at his mother or father?

"All of us, and that includes me and all the counselors, are guilty of all those things, aren't we? Don't bother nodding your heads. You know it and I know it and, most important of all, God knows it. And that's the whole trouble.

"God can't show love to us because He can't stand what we are! God is pure, holy, and righteous. He can't stand sin! He won't let us into heaven with Him because heaven is such a clean, good place that He doesn't want anyone in there that has ever lied, cheated, or stolen. That leaves you and me in a pretty tough spot.

"But, if God loves us so much, do you think He is going to leave us in a spot like that?

"Remember the verse we learned this afternoon? Who can say it?"

Several voices started to say it and stumbled on the unfamiliar words. Jaime remembered the page and in the fading light read aloud: "'For God so loved the world that He gave His only Son. Whoever puts his trust in God's Son will not be lost, but will have life that lasts forever.'"

"That's right! That's the one. Now let's all say it together: 'For God so loved—'"

As the voices repeated the verse Jaime thought, *But that's silly. Everybody dies. Everybody, including you, Mr. Lito. I wonder how smart they really are? They are smart about a lot of things, but they can't be real smart if they talk about things like never dying.*

"Now what kind of life do you think He is talking about? That I will live in this body forever and live to be thousands of years old? No, He is talking about when this body dies the me that lives inside it will go on living with Him in heaven.

"But I just said you and I can't get into heaven! Something's crazy around here. Either you can or you can't. Let's make up our minds.

"'For God so loved the world that He gave His only Son.' Gave Him for what? God gave *Him* to die instead of *us,* having to die because we are bad. If He took our punishment, then that means He took our sins too. You know what that means? That means we don't have any sins anymore; He took them all. Whoopee!! We gonna get to heaven!

"Aren't we? Huh? What's that? You say you still haven't felt God's love for you? Hey! Something's wrong. Maybe we better read a little more and see if we can't find out what. Let's see — 'Whoever puts his trust in God's Son will not be lost, but will have life that lasts forever.' Oh, oh. There it is. 'Whoever puts his trust in God's Son —' That's the hitch.

"You're not gonna get Jesus to take your sins away for you unless — *unless* — unless *you* put your trust in Him.

"And that ain't easy. You gotta really believe that He is alive now; you have to make Him the boss of your life; you have to admit that you are a sinner; and you have to ask Him to come live in your heart. That's what it means to trust in Him.

"Each one of you can do that. And when you do, a new life starts up inside of you. He actually comes into your heart and lives inside you and gives you the power to live the kind of life He wants you to."

No thank you, thought Jaime, *I want to live my life my way. Besides, I don't believe you, Mr. Lito, nobody can live inside me. You guys are plenty smart, but that's too much. That's too far out.*

"Now when any of you guys want to do it, you have to come right up here in front of all the others and do it out loud. Because until you can, you don't really trust in Him. Yes, I'm making it tough for you. When you get home and you tell your mama and she laughs at you, or when you tell your buddies that you won't go steal with them because you got Jesus in your heart and they beat you up — then it is gonna be even harder. You gotta be sure or it ain't no good.

Remember you can't fool God. He knows just exactly what is going on in your heart.

"Maybe some of you are ready to do it, because you talked to some of our gospel teams in Manila, but I'm not gonna ask you to do it now. I want you to think it over and be sure.

"In closing, remember this one thing: Love, God's love, is everywhere. It is in the hearts of the staff and counselors. We all have asked Jesus into our hearts, all of us, the nurse, the cooks, the helpers, all of us, and we want to share it with you.

"Let us pray —"

On the way back to the cabin, Jaime was thinking things out. *Was it really God's love or was it all show? Lesson number two was: Be nice. Lesson number three was: Don't hold grudges. Now if I put them together I got a thing that looks like love. Let me try it out. I ain't got much to lose.*

"Hey, Luis," he said, making sure Art could hear, "if you really want that top bunk, you can have it. It's not right I should fight you for it."

"No, no, friend Jaime, you keep it. It's a small thing. I shouldn't have done it."

Jaime was elated at the smile on Art's face. *Ha, Ha,* he thought. *I fooled him! He thinks I show love. He's not so smart.*

7

The road was dusty and the sun hot. The crowd following Jaime was getting closer and closer. He looked back at them. They were close enough for him to see their sick and twisted bodies. Open sores, twisted backs, pus-filled eyes, crippled legs, but sick as they were, still they gained on him. If only the dust were not so thick, he could run faster. "Jaime! Jaime!" they called. He could not lift his legs out of the dust. They were about to overwhelm him. "Go away!" he shouted, "Go away. I can't help you! Go away!" The dust got deeper — they got closer — one reached out and grabbed him!

"Wake up, you sleepyhead!" Art shook his shoulder. "Don't you wake when you're called?"

Jaime blinked up at Art for just a moment then jumped back and looked around wildly. The panic of the dream changed into fear of the army. But all he saw was Art's smiling face and the same boys as last night. Reassured, he slipped down out of his bunk and stood with the rest.

"Let's go! You got just fifteen minutes to wash your face, brush your teeth, comb your hair, and be back here lined up in front of the cabin. Now move it!"

After much jostling and shoving at the wash basins they

74

were all back at the cabin fairly well washed and combed within the time limit.

Art and Ernie briefly explained the flag-raising ceremony and lined them up according to height. A bugle sounded from near the meeting place.

"Now let's all march over there quietly. Ernie will lead you to our place on the field. This is not a time for talking."

They filed onto the field, each cabin taking its place. One of the staff had his trumpet in his hand. Two others stood by the flagpole ready to raise the colors. When the movement stopped and all were quiet, Mr. Lito raised his hand.

"Gentlemen, our national anthem!" He brought his hand down and, led by the trumpet, they all started to sing:

Land of the morning, child of the sun returning, With fervor burning, thee do our souls adore. Land dear and holy, cradle of noble heroes, Never shall invaders trample thy sacred shores. Ever within thy skies —

Jaime watched as the sun caught the blue and red of the flag and seemed to glint off the gold on the white field. It filled him with pride. He seldom thought about his country and flag, but he realized how much they meant to him. He might be a thief, but above all he was a Filipino. Fingers of pride crawled up and down his back, and he stood a little straighter.

After the last notes of the song drifted away and the flag gracefully responded to the breeze at the top of the pole, there was a moment of silence.

Mr. Lito finally broke it. "Beautiful, isn't it?" He pulled his eyes away from the flag and addressed the boys.

"Today we are going to start out with something new. We call it *crafts.* That means we are going to make something. One of the first things we are going to make is a kite. Each cabin will make a kite. There will be prizes for the most beautiful kite, the best flying kite, the —

A gasp went up from all the boys as the mess hall bell started to ring. It could not be true, could it? Eat so early in the day? And again at dinner and at supper? *Three* times in one day?

"There goes the bell again!" Mr. Lito acted annoyed. "It's always interrupting me. Now I *know* you don't want to eat. I know you would rather stand here and listen to me talk, wouldn't you?"

The boys remembered the day before. "No, no, let's eat. Let's eat!" they yelled.

"You would rather eat rather than listen to me?"

"Yes!!!"

"OK, OK! Let's eat. March over by cabins, quietly and without running, and we will talk about crafts later."

Inside there were platters of scrambled eggs and *tinapa* fish and mounds of rice and juice to drink and the ever present *pandasal.* Three times they would eat. Three times every day. That was the overriding thought of Jaime and every other boy at the camp. They would not misbehave, they would obey every rule they could think of, just so they could eat like that.

With his stomach full, Jaime wandered out to the lawn. He drifted over to some of his cabinmates. As soon as Art came out they made a beeline for him. He was their focal point, their center. They would never be any farther from him than they could help.

Jaime listened to them for awhile as they all tried to seek favor with him. They hung on every word and kept trying to get closer to him. That kind of turned Jaime off. *He shows them a little attention and they fall all over him,* he thought. *I'm glad I don't need that stuff. I'm glad I can make it on my own without falling for that phony love stuff. Look at them — making up to Art as if he was-was — well, some sort of a big hero, or something. I don't need that. I know better. I depend on me. No one else.*

Jaime lifted his head at the faint sound of the carpenter's hammer.

"Hey, Art, can I go over and talk to the carpenters for a minute?"

"OK, but don't be long. We go to crafts soon."

When he came around the garage he saw the wall he had helped with yesterday. Pride washed over him. He laughed at his own reaction, but he felt just a little bigger and maybe a little cleaner for having done something worthwhile.

"Good morning, sirs," he said, acting out lesson number two, be nice.

"Good morning to you, young fellow. Are you back here to help?"

"I only have a few minutes, but I sure would like to."

"Fine. Mr. Torre just knocked over that keg of nails. If you would pick them up then he could get back to work doing something useful." Both men laughed good-naturedly at the jab. "I'm Mr. Mendieta. What's your name?"

"Jaime Jorka." He answered absently. His attention was on the nails. They were clean and bright and *straight*. He had never seen so many like that before! Lovingly he picked them up and carefully put them back in the small keg. His hands almost put them in his pockets, but visions of steaming rice and mounds of bread kept him honest.

"You like nails?" Mr. Torre asked quietly.

"At home — when I want to fix something on our shack — in Tondo — we have to stea — I mean scrounge nails where we can, and they are bent and rusty and — I don't have a hammer anymore and with a rock its so hard to — " He blushed in embarrassment. Those men were professionals and he was telling about his pitiful little attempts at carpentry.

The two men exchanged glances. Mr. Mendieta nodded.

"Well, then, I guess it's time you learned how to drive a nail the right way." Mr. Torre held out his hammer to Jaime.

For a moment he could not believe it. *He knows I'm a thief. Isn't he afraid I will steal it? But, no, I won't. Not here.* He looked up at Mr. Torre. He was looking back at him with a slight smile.

"Here, take it. Now the first thing you have to learn is how to hold your hammer. You hold it down here at the end —" Patiently Mr. Torre led Jaime through all the steps in how to drive a nail. How to hold the hammer. How to swing the hammer. How to hit the nail and not your thumb. And how to straighten the nail when it bent a little. Soon he let Jaime try his hand at nailing the sheeting on the walls.

"This will be covered up with the siding so it doesn't mind if the nails are a little crooked. You gotta learn somewhere." Again the men laughed. It seemed to Jaime that those men were always laughing or chuckling at something.

In the thrill of learning, Jaime, of course, lost all track of time. A sudden hand on his shoulder made him leap and twist out from under it.

"Jaime, I told you to only spend a few minutes here. Come on now. We're late for crafts." Art's frown sent a shaft of fear into Jaime's heart. Mr. Mendieta came to his rescue.

"Art, if he is going to learn to paste something together in that crafts thing, why not you let him stay here and help us and learn how to do something worthwhile? Besides, we need the help if we gonna get this thing done the way you want."

"But the cabin works together on the projects. It wouldn't

79

be right for one guy to —" Art suddenly stopped. He looked at Jaime, and at the men, and then at the job. It seemed forever to Jaime. "Do you want to stay here, Jaime?"

"Yes." Jaime nodded. "I would like very much to."

"OK. But be back at the cabin at nine-thirty sharp, y' hear?"

"Sure thing, Art. Sure thing. Thank you very much." Jaime's breath came out in one long *whoosh*. He did not realize how long he had been holding it. As Art turned and left, Mr. Torre spoke up.

"You asked for it, Jaime. Now you gonna *work* for us. No more play. I don't know if you ever have a job before, but you got one now. First thing, bring those two-by-fours over there to these saw horses—" And work Jaime did. He carried boards. He got nails. He held the end of the tape when the men measured. He fetched tools. And he learned. As the men gave him orders they also explained what they were doing. They took a real delight in their new apprentice and his eagerness to learn.

All too soon it was 9:30.

"You better go now. Don't be late or Art won't let you come back next time. We gonna finish this thing this week with your help, praise the Lord!"

Jaime was thunderstruck. "Are you men missionaries too?"

"No. We just carpenters."

"How come then you talk like them?"

"We praise the Lord just like they do because we believe in Jesus just like they do. You don't have to be a missionary or a preacher to believe in Jesus. He's for everybody. Now hurry, or you be late."

"OK. OK. I go." He started off somewhat dazed by this new turn of events. Suddenly he remembered lesson number two, be nice. He turned back. "Thank you very much for what you teach me. I'll be back as soon as I can. Goodbye."

Just ordinary carpenters, huh? I'll bet. Jaime's thoughts raced with his feet on the way back to the cabin. *Those guys get all sorts of missionaries here just so no matter who we talk to we will always get the same story. They sure want to get us. I wonder if they get some money or something if they get us to ask for Jesus in our hearts. He can't come into our hearts anyway. Our heart's just a pump. I read that somewhere. It's in our heads He would have to come. But those carpenters weren't missionaries. They were Filipinos just like me. Missionaries come from someplace else. But they act like —*

"Here I am on time!" He joined the boys just as they were sitting down under "their tree" in back of the cabin.

"Hey! You miss all the fun!" Poi's enthusiasm bubbled over. "You should see the kite we are going to make. It's big and red and blue and will have a tail that long." He almost lost his grip on his Bible as he flung his arms wide.

Jaime's eyes closed a little, and his lip started to curl as he thought of the *useful* work *he* had done. He caught himself just in time.

"That's good, Poi. I bet you have lot of fun." He could not help noticing the relieved look on Art's face. You almost blew that, Jaime boy, he thought. *If you don't remember the lessons, you are going to get in trouble.*

Art opened his Bible. "Today we are going to study a little bit of the reason *why* we need to have Jesus in our lives and why we don't have Him all the time. So let's turn to page three twenty-four. This is a letter written to the church in the city of Rome about nineteen hundred years ago. Let's see if it doesn't sound like Manila today."

As they read through the first chapter of Romans, Jaime again got that skin-crawling feeling as he recognized the crime and degradation of Tondo in the description of Rome. There was *something* about that Book and about those people that got to him. There was a ring of truth to what they said, but yet it was all wrong. How could they be true and wrong at the same time? He would have to listen more carefully. Learn more. Then maybe he would understand. One thing he knew: he would *have* to understand.

After study was swimming. And after swimming was lunch. Ah! What a lunch! Then more study and reading. Then a new game — softball! Jaime had read of it, but there was never room anywhere in Tondo to play it. Most of the other boys had not played either, so Jaime was not very far behind. Throwing came easy; basketball playing helped there.

But using the bat was all new, and it took a bit of coaching. Art was very good at the game and soon had the whole cabin, including Ernie's half, playing pretty well for a bunch of beginners.

"No, Rudy," he shouted, "You don't catch the ball by putting your hands over your head and ducking. Make a basket out of your fingers, like this, and hold it there."

Jaime got up to bat and hit the ball. He was so surprised he just stood there and watched it.

"Run, Jaime! Run to first base!" He did as he was told and stood there and watched the fielder chase the ball. He stood there and watched the second baseman miss the catch. And he stood there and watched the pitcher pick it up, drop it, and pick it up again. By that time Art, who had been yelling: "Run! — Now stop! —Now run" as the events unfolded on the field, was just standing there with his face in his hands and his shoulders shaking. Jaime was not quite sure whether he was laughing or crying.

Luis was up next. He hit a dribbling grounder right between the legs of the pitcher, through the hands of the second baseman, out into center field where the fielder kicked it before picking it up. Jaime ran to the next base as he had been told, and stopped there. Luis had other instructions (or something) and never slowed rounding first.

"Run, Jaime, run!" Art yelled. Jaime started running just as Luis got to second and the two of them arrived at third in a dead heat. The ball, meanwhile, was wandering around the field, from a throw to a miss, to a fumble. The rival coach was shouting instructions and adding very nicely to the confusion.

"Go back, go back!" Art instructed. So, Jaime and Luis both went back to second. When they got there they realized they had done something wrong. So they discussed it.

"Maybe you should stay here and I go to third," Jaime suggested.

"Better yet, why don't you go all the way home and I stop at third."

"Good idea. Let's."

Again the parade started to third. By that time the pitcher had the ball, and he was not about to throw it anywhere for fear it would get lost. He started to chase the boys, unknown to them. They reached third, Luis stopped, the pitcher bumped into him, dropped the ball, and Jaime ran on home to the cheers of his team.

Art was sitting on the ground holding his sides, tears of laughter rolling down his cheeks. Jaime went up to him.

"This is fun. We do it again sometime, huh?"

"Oh, Jaime, I'm not sure I could stand it!" Art was still shaking with spasms of laughter as he got the game going again.

Jaime had one more turn at bat, but he struck out much to the disappointment of all. Art was really interested to see what Jaime would do when he got on base again.

During the afternoon craft session Jaime went back to

work with the carpenters. That time he learned about headers and lintels and jambs as they framed in the windows and doors. When he was not busy fetching something or carrying boards, the men gave him some scraps of wood and let him practice sawing. With those they were stern taskmasters. He had to saw right on the mark and straight and square. Wood cost money and there was never any to waste. A nail could be straightened and re-driven, but if a board was cut wrong there was little way it could be fixed. At first the saw never wanted to go straight, but under the expert advice of the men he slowly improved. By the end of the session he could almost make the saw stay on the marks.

"Now you take those scraps of wood up to the kitchen. They can use them in the stove. You got them all cut up so they don't have to split them any." Mr. Mendieta chuckled.

Jaime had been a little afraid to ask them anything about Christianity. He was not sure why, but having "ordinary" people Christians was getting a little close to home. He watched their actions and speech. He noticed many things, such as, they never got mad at him no matter how badly he goofed up, they were always kidding and joking with each other, and once in a while even with him; also, they never swore. Jaime did once when he got a splinter in his hand. All they did was look at him and shake their heads. That had more effect than a beating.

That night at the meeting a fellow by the name of Reverend Max talked to them. He was a little different from Mr.

Lito. Not quite as free and easy or as funny. But the message was the same. God's love and how it can change your life. How it can change you from a thief, liar, and no-good to an honest, considerate, loving person.

"You have been studying this Book —" he held the Bible high "— and I know some of you have believed and want to give your heart to Jesus. Now is the time, my friends. Right now. We will bow our heads and pray, and if there are any of you who want to take that step, just raise your hand and I will see it. Then you can come forward and we will give you the chance to tell all the others about it. Remember it says in the book of Romans, chapter ten, verse nine: 'If you say with your mouth that Jesus is Lord, and believe in your heart that God raised Him from the dead, you will be saved from the penalty of sin,' Let us bow our heads and pray—"

When he got to the point where he asked them to raise their hands, Jaime could not resist taking a peek. He saw a few hands go up on the other side of the group. Then he heard a sob from someone close. He looked over, and there was Poi, with his hand held high and tears running down his cheeks.

Contempt curled up inside him. He did not even pretend anymore to have his head bowed. He looked up and around at all the others that had raised their hands. Most of them were crying or trying hard not to. *Oh no!* he thought. *What a bunch of sissies! A guy fills them with a lot of hot air*

*and they cry like a bunch of babies. Not for this guy. I got
more brains than to fall for that. A big emotional buildup to
do something that don't make sense.*

One after the other the boys came forward. They went
up to the front and each one said some little thing like: "I
want you to come into my heart, Jesus, and take away all
my badness." Or, "Jesus, I been bad. I'm a sinner. Come
into me now." Most of them could not finish before they
broke down and started to cry. The longer that went on the
more disgusted Jaime got.

How can they be so foolish! he thought. *How can they
believe that someone who has been dead all these years will
come inside them and change them all around? What is
this except some part of a big make-believe something that
just hooks people into going to church and giving away all
their money? Nothin' like that can ever change me. I'm a
thief a liar, and a tough guy that's gonna get out of Tondo
on his own.*

From somewhere down deep inside him, the thought
came almost like a voice: *Oh, yeah? Thief? Then why didn't
you steal those nails when you had the chance? They never
would have caught you. Liar? Why did you tell them about
using a rock on the nails? You could have lied about that
easy enough. For a tough guy you have been awfully nice
lately — Ha, ha, ha! They're getting to you, Jaime!*

*No! No, they're not! I'll show them! It's dumb, dumb,
dumb! I won't fall for that stuff I only do it so they will feed*

me. So I can learn how to act good. And learn how to be a carpenter Jaime's world was starting to tilt, but he fought hard in his mind and slowly brought it into balance again. *It's dumb, dumb, dumb,* he thought.

But he was shaken, very, very shaken.

8

The next morning he was still worried. He liked the lessons he was learning. They seemed to be the right thing, but could he use them without going soft? Would he stay tough enough to make it in Tondo? It was during the basketball game they played that day that he got it all straightened out.

Everybody knew how to play basketball. They played it all the time in Tondo. He thought for a moment of Rio and how he would have enjoyed it, but those thoughts were quickly swallowed up by the interest of playing on a full-sized court. Luis turned out to be as good a player as Jaime, and the two teamed up and became a tough combo to beat.

After about a half hour of practice they started a game; Art's bunch against Ernie's. Jaime took over as captain and no one questioned.

"Luis, you be center, you're tallest. Rudy, you and I be forwards; Pat and Manual, guards; and Poi, you kinda hang around our basket and break up any plays that come down there. Let's go!"

With Luis' skill as a shooter and Jaime's direction as captain they soon outdistanced the others. Jaime started out the game by driving really hard, but after getting caught in a few fouls he slowed down and started playing more carefully. He did not foul when the referee was looking —

and was overly polite when he helped an opponent to his feet. Luis noticed what Jaime was doing and soon started in himself.

"So sorry, my fren," he would say as he helped a boy up. The "friend" would glare at him, knowing there was nothing he could do about it because the referee did not catch it. Soon the other team got tired of that and started to hit back. Jaime and Luis never lost their cool, but played it for all it was worth — always helping and polite, and making the other team look bad. As they got angrier, the other team became less cautious in their revenge, and Jaime and Luis collected many free throws. They grinned at each other as the score mounted in their favor.

That's the smart way, Jaime thought. *Luis and I are a couple of smart fellows. We know how to make the rules pay off. And that's smart. I'm not getting soft. I'm getting smart. I'll play the lessons I'm learning here the same way I play the rules in this game. Ha! I'll show them!*

In his exuberance he drove for the basket a little too hard and got whistled down. Luis frowned at him.

"Sorry, my fren." He shrugged his shoulders at him. "You can't win 'em all."

After the game and a quick swim to cool off, Art led them to their regular study spot by the palm tree in back of the cabin. Jaime sat next to Luis rather off by himself.

He smiled at his new friend. Luis returned it. Jaime's thoughts were far back in Manila when Art opened the lesson.

"This time turn to page three forty-six. This is chapter

thirteen of the letter. Paul, one of the leaders of the early church, wrote to some Christians living in the city of Rome. He is talking about—"

Art's voice faded out of Jaime's mind as he thought of the possibilities of teaming up with Luis when they got back to Manila. Instead of a stupid partner like Rio, a smart partner would bring in a lot more money. If Jaime applied some of the lessons he had learned here at camp, he could keep things under control so Luis would not take over the whole thing. *He's smart enough,* he thought, *to see the benefit of a full partnership rather than just one being boss. We could get some other fellows and lead them. When we got enough for me to leave and get out, he would have a full, operating gang and wouldn't mind me leaving —*

"— that way the police can't get you so you don't have to be afraid."

The word "police" caught Jaime's attention and he started to read the text they were studying. "Every person must obey the leaders of the land. There is no power given but from God, and those who do right do not have to be afraid of the leaders. Those who do wrong are afraid of them. Do you want to be free from fear of them? Then do what is right. You will be respected instead." *Ha,* he thought, *not in Tondo. In Tondo you would be dead from starvation. If you want real respect there you got to be smart enough not to get caught.*

He watched Art as he taught. *The guy really believes all*

91

that stuff, he thought. *Art, you are a nice guy but your head is not where it is at. Even the police don't obey the rules. Come live with me for a while and I will show you a few things. And so will Luis. We know where things are at, and they are not like that Book says. Maybe, Mr. Art, you are not quite as smart as I thought you were.*

That night at the meeting Mr. Lito got really wound up. They had a movie and he had put on a good magic show. So by the time he got to the message, the boys were all on the edge of their seats, listening to every word he said. Jaime and Luis sat together enjoying their newfound friendship. Jaime had not approached Luis on his partnership idea yet, feeling it was not quite time.

"Fellas, we both know what the streets are like because we both been there. I put my time in on the garbage can detail, just like you. How many miles you run from the police? I bet I run a hundred. How many times you have your guts tied up in knots wonderin' if your 'buddy' was gonna squeal? Or wonderin' if they were gonna believe your lie and let you go. We both know what that side's like.

"But here's one place you ain't been that I have. And that's the other side. I tell you, until you try it, you don't know what good is. You are going it alone now. But you get Jesus in your heart and you're not alone. How can you be? Isn't Jesus *in* you? If He's in you, He is with you. And if He's with you, you're not alone. Right? Any dummy can figure that out. Can't you? And Jesus said He would never leave you. Nothin' can separate you from Him. Anybody else you know ever say that? And mean it?

"I'm not gonna fill you guys with a lot of baloney. You're too smart for that. You say: Sure, I accept Jesus, and I stop stealing and cheating, and then you know what happens? I start starving. No, my friends, Jesus don't leave you to starve. Like I say, He helps you. How? I can't tell each one of you how He will do it. Me, He got going on magic shows. Raymond there," he pointed to a counselor, "he got a job working on jeepneys. Juan, there, he got into junk — that is, dealing in junk — made enough money to go back to school to be a preacher. I don't know just what is gonna happen to you, but I know Jesus not gonna leave you alone to starve.

"Now is the time, my friend. You know what to do. Confess you need Him and ask Jesus to come into your heart to stay. You can't beat it."

Not now, thank you, friend Lito, Jaime thought. *Now I got something better. Now I got a smart guy for friend and we gonna be partners. We gonna get that big gang and we gonna make plenty money.* With a confident smile Jaime looked over at Luis.

In dumbfounded shock he watched as Luis, his eyes shining and fixed on Mr. Lito, got up from his seat and went forward to the platform.

No, No, No! Jaime's mind screamed at Luis. *Don't do it! We had it made! It would be so good!* He slumped back

93

in his seat, bitterness boiling up through him. *Dumb, dumb, dumb. Stupid, dumb. All of them. Luis, Mr. Lito, even Art. All dumb.*

He crouched down farther into his seat as waves of bitterness swept over him. The familiar old dull ache came back, and he nursed it carefully until it was a hot flame. That feeling had been gone the last few weeks, and he had not realized how much he had missed it. He would show them, he would show them. Familiar phrases, familiar thoughts. To think he almost fell for all that stuff they were feeding him here — but he would show them. He spent the rest of the evening reviving his old dreams and ignoring the actions around him.

They had almost reached the cabin on the way back from the meeting when Art reached out for Jaime. As usual, Jaime twisted away, but Art said, "I want to talk with you a minute, Jaime." To the others he said: "You go on to the cabin. Ernie has some songs he wants to teach you."

Soon after they were seated on a log Art said, "OK, Jaime, what's up?"

"What you mean, 'What's up?'"

"You know. Something happened at that meeting tonight. I know you well enough to see it, and you know me well enough to tell me."

"I don't think I want to."

"Don't be sullen. Out with it."

Jaime looked at Art for a long minute. His jaw was

clenched. Suddenly he said, "Art, you're dumb."

"Oh?"

"Yeah. I once thought you pretty smart, but now I don't think so. Now I think you're dumb."

"Why?"

"You know a lot of things from books; you been to a lot of schools, but you don't know real life. Maybe you do know and are a liar, but I don't think so. You say you believe all the stuff you teach here. If you really believe, you are dumb."

"Keep talkin'."

"It's that love stuff. All Jesus stuff built on love. Look, it's OK to *act* like you love people, but to believe, to really *believe* in it is dumb because people take you for all you got when you do. They walk on you."

"They do?"

"How can you be so dumb to ask that question? You are dumb, dumb, dumb!"

"As I told you before, Jesus told me to go out and help people the same way people helped me. And I want to help you. Haven't you been helped here at camp?"

"Yeah. But you don't do it just 'cause you love me. You like to brag about how many you help."

"That's not true. It's just because of Jesus' love."

"Oh, sure, I bet you." Jaime became foolish in his conceit. "Hey, I tell you somethin', then see how much you love me. Remember you get robbed in Quinta Market? Yeah, well I'm the guy who did it. Now, how much you love me?"

95

A wistful smile came on Art's lips. He slowly reached into his pocket.

"I was wondering how I would ever be able to return this to you. I guess this is as good a time as any." He handed Jaime his wooden name tag. "It was broken. I glued it together as best I could."

Jaime stared at Art, his mouth half open. His breath came faster and faster as the truth sank in. "You —you — really — do love me." A burning started at the back of his eyes, and his breath caught in his throat and came out as sob. "No!" he screamed. "No!" He got up and blindly ran away.

In his wild running, Jaime came to the construction site. Out of breath, he sank down on a pile of lumber. His thoughts were all mixed up. *He knew all the time. He could have put me in jail. But he helped me. He should have put me in jail. But he loved me. That's stupid. No, it's not. I'd be in jail. How can he love me? I robbed him and he knew it. Is that stupid? He couldn't love me. How could he? He said Jesus loves me through him!*

He looked up into the night sky as if trying to see God, trying to see if it was true. Tears blurred the stars and rolled down his cheeks.

The crushing thought came: *I — the guy who thought he was so smart — I am the one who is stupid. They really do believe and practice Jesus' love.*

He knelt in the sawdust alongside the lumber. The smell

of the wood reminded him that Jesus had been a carpenter.

"Hey, Jesus." His prayer was simple and direct. "Art was right and I was wrong. I confess to You." He confessed the worst thing he could think of. "I was stupid. I was real — real dumb, and I ask You to come into my heart or head or whatever You doooo —" The last was a long sob as the peace of God settled in his soul and he knew he had been truly forgiven. He knelt there quietly crying as he let the tightness inside relax. It was as if Christ's hand on his shoulder was drawing the hurt and evil out of him and filling him with peace. He drew deep breaths of air. The knot of anger was gone, and he filled the space with clean night air. "Thank You, Jesus. Thank You, Jesus. Thank You," he repeated over and over.

He felt a real hand on his shoulder, and that time he did not pull away. He recognized it as a true touch of love.

"Oh, Art." He tried manfully, but unsuccessfully, to stop the flow of tears. "He forg-g-gave m-me for being s-stupid. That's p-pretty good, isn't it?" Jaime smiled through his tears.

"Oh, Jaime, He's a wonderful God." Art knelt beside him and they laughed and wept together.

The way the news spread over camp, one would have thought they put out a newspaper. Everybody seemed to know that Jaime Jorka had accepted Christ. The serving boys in the mess hall smiled and gave him an extra portion. Evelyn Rivera, the nurse, called from her office as he went by: "Hi, there, new young Christian." Mr. Torre and Mr. Mendieta called him "brother" when he showed up on the job. The reaction of the boys depended upon whether or not they had come to Christ yet. Those that had come welcomed him either shyly or openly, depending on their dispositions. Those that had not sort of ignored the whole thing. Poi and Luis and himself got together and talked it over a little, but they were all so new at it they found it hard to put into words. But when Pat and Manual joined them that night, the words started to flow.

"Poor Rudy, he doesn't have a chance," stated Luis. "With all us praying for him, Jesus gonna find him even if he don't find Jesus." They all laughed at that and kept on praying. The next to the last night their prayers were answered, and Rudy joined them.

It was Mr. Torre who brought Jaime back down to earth.

"Jaime, what you gonna do when you get back to Manila?"

"Do? I'm gonna tell others how good Jesus is. What else?"

"No, no. I mean how you gonna make a living? I hear tell you once were a pretty good thief. But now what you do now when you can't steal?"

Jaime looked at him in confusion. He had not thought about that at all.

"We wondered," Mr. Mendieta said, "if you think you could learn to shine shoes?"

"I-I guess so. But I don't have a shine box or the stuff to shine with."

"But look at all these scraps of lumber we got around here." Mr. Torre's twinkling eyes gave away the fact that it was not a new idea. "I bet we could make a shine box outa all this stuff. Specially if the young fellow making it will listen to his elders and cut the wood and nail it the way they tell him."

"I will! I will!" Jaime jumped at the idea.

"Hey, Mr. Torre, you notice how our cool, tough young man suddenly act all the time happy? You think maybe something happen to him?"

"Oh, Mr. Mendieta," Jaime said with mock seriousness, "terrible thing happened. I can't find my heart anymore. It's gone."

"Gone for good?"

"Yep. A fellow named Jesus took it and now I am happy all the time!" They all laughed with him.

"But I do have a lot to do." Jaime became serious. "I've been bad for so long I'll have to show Jesus that I can be good, to show Him I really mean it, before I can expect Him to do anything for me."

The two men exchanged glances. Mr. Mendieta spoke first. "Maybe you better talk to Art about that before you try too much. You don't have to 'show' Jesus — He knows. He's ready to help you right away. He's with you all the time. Right here. Maybe Art can tell you what or how He does it. All I know is that He is ready to help you anyway.

"But talking about help, we better get on with helping you with the shine box or we not gonna get it done."

Mr. Torre pulled a sketch out of his pocket. "I just *happen* to have the plans for a shine box here with me. It's gonna be a little harder than sawing planks for a wall. There are some angles that gotta be cut just so. Now this," he held up an L-shaped piece of metal about two feet long on a side, "is a carpenter's square. With it you can lay out those angles —"

It was harder, but Mr. Torre was a patient and exact teacher, and soon they had a pretty good looking shine box with carrying rope and all. They even found some paint, and Jaime proudly painted an ichthus, or fish symbol, on it like the one that was on Art's wallet.

"Here is some brown polish, but you will need a brush, a rag, some black, and some white polish at least before you can get going." Mr. Mendieta admired the finished product.

"I got a little money hidden at home — but wait, I gotta give that back to Art." Jaime was learning restitution. "I just need a little bit to get going. After that I can buy some."

By the time he left camp he was fully outfitted. Evelyn gave him some white polish. Art had some black. A rag was easy to find, and an old but serviceable shoe brush showed up from someplace in the headquarters building. He even had a chance to practice on Art a few times.

"Oh, boy! Am I ever gonna show Jesus what a good kid can be. No more fights, no more stealing, no more swearing, no more bad thoughts — even about my parents — and my sisters. Oh, Art! I wanna be so good that He will want to use for His work alla time!" Jaime's enthusiasm bubbled out in all sorts of wild promises.

"Wait a minute, Jaime. Wait a minute. You don't have to show Jesus how good you are. He knows. After all, He made you that way. You have to depend on Him to show you how to do what He wants. Don't try to do it in your own strength. You can't."

"You wanna bet? I'm gonna!" The same determination and drive Jaime had to get out of Tondo was now directed to "show Jesus" what he could do for Him. All of Art's talks about depending on Jesus for strength fell on deaf ears.

"Jesus gotta use people to do His work, right?" Jaime argued. "So I'm gonna be a good people so I can be used to do His work. That's that."

"But He wants a servant, someone who will do what He wants."

"That's right. And what He wants is good people. So I am gonna be good."

"But the Lord — OK, Jaime, go to it. Just remember, you have the Holy Spirit in you, and He will teach you all things about Jesus. We'll give Him time to work in you — or on you — and then get going on a gospel team or something. OK?"

"OK, Art." Jaime laughed with the joy of fellowship. "We get together real soon."

When the bus got back to Manila, the Lord's newest young lamb headed happily and confidently off into the mud and shanty jungle he called home.

9

"Gimme dat!"

Jaime's catlike reflexes saved him. The blow glanced off his shoulder and his father staggered past him, carried by the force of his blow.

"Where you been? Where you steal that shine box? Gimme it!"

Jaime found it easy to stay out of the reach of the staggering drunk trying to get him. For the first time, pity rather than anger welled up inside him. He was barely aware of the giggles of the crowd that had gathered to watch the spectacle.

"Now, Papa, now, Papa, if you take it and sell it now you just get one bottle. But I keep it and make money, and I be able to give you lots of money."

"Money! Money! Where you get that money? Don't you hide any money again. You hear!"

"What you mean 'hide money'? — Oh, no!" Jaime turned and ran for home, ignoring the curses and shouts of his father.

"Jaime, you no-good! Where you been? You leave us whole week, you pig. What we do for money? You rotten — " His mother's curses followed him as he raced around the shack into his lean-to.

"Where you get that shine box? Where you been? We need money!" His mother's shrieking was ignored as he looked at the wreck of his lean-to. The mattress had been all torn up, some boards were knocked loose, and there was a gaping hole where the money had been hidden. For a moment the old anger started up inside him. "No, Jesus, I won't get mad. I won't get mad. They need the money, but I bet Papa get it all. That no-good — No, Jesus, I won't get mad. I won't!"

Mama yanked on the shine box rope, pulling him backward out of the lean-to.

"What you got here?" She started to paw through the things in the box. "We sell this and get some money."

"No, Mama, no. I use this to shine shoes and make lots of money." He grabbed the things back from her and scrambled to his feet. He had to escape.

"Where you been? Where you get that box? If you steal it, you sell it and bring home money!"

"No, Mama, I been to a — a ca —" he knew she would not understand. "I been to a place where I learn to shine shoes. I learn lots of other things. I want to tell you —" He was backing away as he talked. Mama was reaching for him, her face twisted with anger. It was no time to talk. He turned and ran.

He stopped a few blocks away when it was safe. He looked up to the sky and prayed. "Jesus, that wasn't exactly lying. I did learn to shine shoes there. But thank You most that I learn about You. I'll show You, I'll be good. They were right when they said it's gonna be hard when we get back." A wry chuckle escaped him. "Only been back ten minutes and get hit by Papa, robbed of my money, and yelled at by Mama. I wonder where my sisters are? That's OK, Jesus — I don't really need them now." With spirits lifted by the moment of prayer, he looked around. *Well,* he thought, *I guess I better get busy and shine some shoes. I'll go down to Quinta Market. That's where this whole mess started.*

He looked for Rio when he passed his box, but he was not there. The market was the same as always. Big and hot and smelly. He walked around trying to decide the best place to start his new career. In the meat and fish section not many people looked as though they wanted a shine. There were mostly women buying what they wanted and then getting out of the smell as soon as they could. The vegetable and fruit sections were not much better. The people there were not in such a hurry, but they were still mostly women. In the hardware, cloth, and curio sections there were many more men and even some tourists. Unfortunately there were also more shine boys.

"Shine, mister, shine?" he called out, mimicking the other boys. "Shine, mister, shine?" The others were getting some business, so he thought he would too.

"Here, boy." A man held up his hand.

Jaime started over, but before he could get there another boy jumped in ahead of him. Jaime pulled back his foot to kick the other when he suddenly remembered Jesus. "OK, OK, Jesus, I won't. At least not this time — no. Not any time. But I — but I — but I will show You how I be good."

The next time a man signaled for a shine, Jaime did not wait. He lunged for the place and swung around so his shine box "accidentally" hit the other boy racing to the job and knocked' him away. *I told Jesus I would be good,* he thought, *and that was pretty good, knocking that guy away like that.*

"You get first class shine, mister." He smiled up at his first customer. The man scowled back. "Yes, sir, first class." He took out him mangy brush and cleaned off the shoe as best as he could. There was some mud caked on one side of the shoe. Jaime had to use his fingernail to scrape it off. *I need a small stiff brush,* he thought, *and maybe some liquid polish to take care of things like that.* Suddenly he noticed the man's shoes were dark red-brown, and he only had light brown polish. *I hope he don't notice,* Jaime thought.

No such luck.

"Hey, kid, how come you use light polish on my dark shoes?"

"Oh, this very good polish — very good. You wait and see."

"I don't know." The man scowled even more.

Jaime rubbed the polish on with his hands, getting it as smooth as he could. He buffed it with the rag, and thought he was doing a pretty good job.

"Hey, kid, you gonna take all day?"

"Wanna do a good job — a good job." *Say anything. Anything to get the money.* Just as Jaime finished the last shoe, the man suddenly kicked at him.

"You no-good bum! Look what you do! You get polish on my sock." The man pointed to the first foot Jaime had done. "I'm not gonna pay you for that lousy job!" The man kicked over Jaime's box and strode off, laughing. Jaime grabbed for his stuff and started to get up, then sank back down on his knees completely dumbfounded.

"Wassa matter, boy, don' you know how-a shine shoe?" The boy he hit laughed.

"Maybe you sell some fish in that fish box, huh?"

"That fish box stink so bad he not pay you?" The other shine boys taunted him, trying to bait him into some action.

Jaime sat there, his eyes staring, his breath panting. He wanted to strike out at anything and everything. The boys were close, and he focused on them. When they saw his look they shut up and drew back. "Jesus—" he prayed, "Jesus — Jesus — look, Jesus, look. I'm gonna show You, really gonna show You I can be good. But do You *have* to make it so hard? Do You have to beat me into the ground the very first day? —I'm sorry, Jesus. That not a very nice thing to say to You. You Boss. Do as You want. But I still gonna show You."

He looked at the boys again. "I show you, too," was all he said. He smiled, got up, and started in again.

"Shine, mister, shine?"

It was late in the afternoon. He had had several shine jobs and the amount of money he had made was not too bad. However, he had to buy a new brush when the old one lost all its bristles, and also had to buy some dark brown polish. At that rate he was not going to have much to take home.

He was trying to figure out how much longer he would have to work when a voice said: "Well, look here! He got out of the army camp and learned how to shine shoes."

"Rio! My fren Rio!" Jaime jumped up in his joy at seeing his friend. "Was not army camp, they teach us all about Jesus! He is wonderful! You gotta know Him. And we play basketball on full-size court. And Jesus gonna help you same as He help me. Listen, I tell —"

Words tumbled out in wild profusion. Jaime did not notice the other boys with Rio until he reached for his old friend.

"Whoa. Slow down, slow down." Rio backed off from Jaime to between the two others. None of the three were smiling. "You go away and leave just like that. Then you come back and think I'm your friend. No. No more am I your friend. Now I got friends of my own." He indicated the boys on each side of him. They looked at Jaime, sneering slightly.

"Well. I — I — that's OK. Now all three of you should hear about Jesus. He make everything OK."

"Stop! Look, Mr. Jesus-man, don't give us that stuff. Like you say once: How Jesus gonna help us? Is He gonna drive up in a big car and hand us out money?" Rio laughed at his own joke. The other two laughed with him even if they did not know what was funny. "We got better things to do with our time than listen to some two-bit Jesus preacher." He turned and walked off with his nose tilted up in a very superior attitude, confident that Jaime would not try anything while he had his two friends to help him.

I could mop the street up with all three of you, Jaime thought. He suddenly realized how he had been gripping his brush, as though it were a weapon. "I'm sorry, Jesus," he prayed. "I shouldn't think thoughts like that, even if we both know it's true. But I will tell them about You, some day. If I don't, who will? I'll show You."

It was dark by the time he got home. He had no idea as to how he would be received. He only had sixty-eight centavos left, and he was afraid that would not satisfy his mama. She would never believe that was all he had, especially after finding the money he had hidden. Just to be on the safe side, he hid his shine box in some bushes about a block from home. He held the money in his hand and pushed open the door.

"Here's the money I made today." He laid it on the table in front of her.

"Gimme it all!" Mama started up from the table. Papa looked at him through his drunken fog.

"That's all I have. I had to buy a brush. I'll make more tomorrow.

"Gimme it all!"

"That *is* all!"

"Lying pig! You hold out some like you always do!"

"No, Mama, not this time. I swear!"

"Pig! Gimme the rest of it or get out!"

"But Mama —"

"Get out! You no-good liar, get out!"

"Yeah — get out. Out, you hear!" Papa lurched to his feet, grasped the empty bottle in front of him by the neck and started to swing it at Jaime like a club.

Jaime got out.

He walked down the street, the retrieved shine box bumping his side, trying to figure out what to do.

He could not go over to Rio's anymore, that was for sure. If he slept out in the open, the police would pick him up, and also he would have to be careful that no one robbed him of his shine box.

He noticed an alley across the street that had some boxes piled in it. Maybe he could get one of those and sleep on the cardboard. He crossed the street, but a dog chained across the alley kept him out. He finally found some newspapers and carefully spread them out on the ground next to a wall of a house. He lay down on them, cuddled up to his shine box, pulled what papers he could over himself, and slept, fitfully dreaming of evening meetings, camp counselors, and full bellies.

10

The ground was hard, and Jaime was stiff and sore by morning. He pulled his box closer and leaned on it as he watched the sky light up. He scrunched up against the side of the house and took his Bible out of the sack. A "quiet time," Art had called it. A time to be quiet and alone with God. When he finished reading the sun was fully up and the day well started.

Remembering lesson number one about being clean, he found a water faucet and washed and brushed as best he could. It was a far cry from Camp Ilaw, but it did make him feel better.

It's funny, he thought, *how fast you can get used to something. 'Specially eating. One of those big camp breakfasts would sure feel good right now.*

"Well, Jesus, I guess that's not how it's gonna be. Whatever way You want it. So I better get busy if I'm gonna get anywhere today. Thank You."

He put away his Bible, slung his shine box over his shoulder and headed for the Quinta Market.

By noon he kind of had the hang of it. Tourists and businessmen were the best bets for customers, and the market was a good place for them. There were a lot of other shine boys there, and the competition was rough at times, but Jaime did OK.

He got a few questions about the design on the side of his box, and he used those as opportunities to tell others of Jesus. Most of the reactions were indifferent. So they asked, so they got an answer, so what. He wished he were better at explaining Jesus. He wished there were some way he could learn. He never thought of going to Art to find out.

It was about noon that another customer asked him about the fish symbol on his box.

"Oh," said Jaime, "that's for Christians."

"Well, what do you have for Muslims? A crescent?"

"I don't know much about that. All I know is Jesus is my Savior and that lets everybody know."

"How?"

"Well, that's the Jesus sign. Those are — er — er — Greek! Yeah, Greek letters. They stand for 'Jesus Christ, God's Son, Savior' and that's who He is."

"Who?"

"Jesus. He is Savior. He saves you."

"From what?"

"From all the bad and stupid things you do and should be punished for and not get to heaven, and it is the best way to be."

The man laughed at Jaime's rush of words. It was a kind laugh, full of good humor. "I didn't think any of you street boys ever believed in Jesus. Look here, son." The man bent over and showed Jaime a small silver outline of a fish he had fastened to the front of his shirt. Jaime had never seen one before.

"What does that mean?"

"Oh, that's for Christians." The man echoed Jaime's words.

"Hey! That's pretty good!" Jaime's grin almost split his face. "I gotta remember now and look for that on other people. I only been a Christian a few days now and I don't know all those things." He finished the shoes and said, "That be fifty centavos."

"Fifty centavos. That's not bad for a shine and a sermon." The man pulled out a small coin purse and started to count out the money. Jaime caught the flicker of motion out of the corner of his eye.

"Stop!" he yelled. Leaping to his feet, he threw a hip block into Rio as he make a running grab for the purse. Alerted by Jaime's yell, the man sidestepped the other boy and held tightly to his purse.

"Grab him! Grab him! He tried to rob me!"

Jaime just stood there and watched Rio scamper to his feet. He gave Jaime one venomous glare of hatred and ran off. Jaime felt a stinging in the back of his eyes as he watched him go. *I feel tears of sadness for Rio,* he thought. *I, of all people, feel sad for Rio, of all people. Oh, Rio!* he cried silently. *There is a better way, a much better way!*

"Why didn't you grab him, boy? You could have. He tried to rob me!"

Jaime shook his head. "No. I couldn't. He used to be my friend."

"I suppose you expect a big tip for stopping them." The man was very displeased.

"Oh, no. Just fifty centavos." Jaime looked at him wide-eyed.

"Humpf. Maybe you are a Christian after all." He handed him sixty centavos and walked off.

"Hey, boy, you got guts." Another shine boy had watched the whole thing. "He gonna come back and get you, for sure. Them guys can be *mean.*"

"Not Rio. He usta be my friend. He knows better than to try to get me. I'm surprised he tried to rob my man. I thought I teach him better than that."

"OK. But don't keep your back turned."

"Don't worry." Jaime was puzzled as to why he was so upset by the robbery. He picked up his box, went over to a stand and bought a loaf of *pandesal* and went out behind the market to eat and think.

He sat down against a wall and looked over the Pasig River. While he munched on the bread he pulled the cloth bag with his personal belongings Out of the shine box and took out his Bible.

"They tell me, Jesus," he prayed, "that everything I gotta know is in here. Maybe You show me what I need now. It bothers me quite a bit that Rio pull robbery on me. Have I changed that much? You got words in here for me?" Jaime had not learned the "amens" or "in His names" yet. He just talked to Jesus.

As he flipped through the pages he remembered something near the front about Jesus' telling people how to act. There it was! Matthew, chapter 5. He read ravenously, the words filling his spiritual hunger.

"You are happy when people act and talk in a bad way to you and make it very hard for you," he read, "and tell bad things and lies about you because you trust in Me. Be glad and full of joy because your pay will be much in heaven."

"Thank You, Jesus. But I don't care too much now about my pay later. What I really want to do is things that please You now."

Later on he read: "But I tell you, do not fight with the man who wants to fight." As usual, the Word of God had a soothing effect on him.

The sun was high and it was in the heat of the day. Business was slow in the market, so he thought he might go home and see what Mama would say today. He had two pesos ten from the morning's work. Maybe that would put her in a better mood.

He was about halfway home when he heard a shout from a group of boys about a block away. He looked up and saw it was Rio and four buddies. They were shaking fists at him and starting to run his way. Rio was out to get his revenge.

"Jesus, You say not to fight, but there are five of them.

They gonna kill me! If I don't fight there is only one thing to do — *run!*" He headed off away from them at a dead run. He should have been able to outdistance them, as quick as he was, but he suddenly realized the shine box was slowing him down.

With a sinking feeling he realized he was going to lose his shine box. If he kept it with him it would slow him down until the boys caught him. They would beat him and take his box. If he left it he would get away but would still lose the box. He was finished.

"Jesus," he gasped out a prayer, "help me. I can't do it!" He climbed up another step on his spiritual ladder. "I need You! I can't do it myself."

He ran around a corner, and there was the alley with the guard dog chained across it. Without even thinking, he jumped over the dog and burrowed down into the pile of boxes. The dog never stirred.

As the boys turned the corner after him the dog leaped to his feet and strained at the chain snarling and barking.

"He not in there!" Rio yelled. "Where he go?"

"Maybe that house! He go over the fence."

"You go there. I go around the next corner." The boys split up, frustrated over losing Jaime. The dog continued to guard the alley, growling and barking whenever any one came close. After the boys disappeared he lay down in his pose of indifference, but was instantly on his feet when Rio and a friend came around the corner.

Rio picked up a stone and threw it at the dog.

"Shut up! You mutt. We not coming in your dirty alley."

Jaime waited until his heart stopped pounding after they left. Now how was he going to get out? "Jesus," he prayed, "I need Your help again. I gotta get out of here. That dog look like he asleep, but You and I know better. What we gonna do?" After a pause, "OK, I get up and leave, just like You say."

He moved a little, shuffling some boxes, making enough noise to alert the dog. It did not move. Slowly Jaime got to his feet. Still no movement. He inched past the dog, as far away from him as he could. The dog never even looked at him. Soon he was out in the street, clear of the alley.

That time he got down on his knees and really prayed. "Thank You, Jesus. Thank You. I been stupid again. I did not listen to Art when he tell me what a good friend You are as well as being God. Now I know what he means when he say You have strength, when he say You have power to help us. I been foolish when I try to show You. I should just wait and let *You* show *me.* Oh, friend Jesus, I'm so glad You show me this. You show me You can take care of me if I just let You." A much different Jaime got up onto his feet. He looked up once more. "Now I know what I gotta do." He slung his shine box over his shoulder and went looking for Rio.

He found him with his two friends at his box. They all jumped to their feet when they saw him coming. They were not sure three-to-one were good odds. Jaime's reputation as a fighter was a good one.

"Take it easy, fellows." He smiled. "I'm not out to get you. That's not Jesus' way. Here, you take this shine box." He slung it off his shoulder and took out his cloth bag. "You learn to shine shoes, not steal. It's better that way.

"Hey! With the three of you, maybe one get customers, one shine shoes, and you, Rio, collect the money! That would work pretty good."

"Why you do this?" Rio recovered first.

Jaime looked him straight in the eye and smiled. "Jesus tell me to. I'll come back later and tell you more about Him." He turned and casually sauntered away.

The boys stood and watched him go. One of them looked down at the box, picked it up, and started to dump it out.

Rio was still watching where Jamie had disappeared. A smile twitched the corners of his mouth. "Hey! Cut that out!" he yelled at the boy. "We maybe use that thing after all."

Jaime headed for ACTION headquarters in San Juan. He wanted to talk to Art about the latest development. Even if Art was not there he could find *some* Christian to talk to. He was surprised how much he missed talking about Jesus.

It was a long way to the headquarters — almost fifteen kilometers. When he was on Shaw Boulevard he was tempted to hitch a ride on the back of a jeepney or truck as he used to. But, no, that was not Jesus' way anymore, he thought.

"Jesus, I'm not trying to show You how good I am anymore, but we should act the way You want, shouldn't we?" His prayer was simple and direct. He mulled that and other questions over in his mind as he walked along. There was so much to learn. There were so many questions he had for Art. *I bet I study for the rest of my life and I still not know everything.* He laughed at the thought of going to school in heaven. He thought of rows of desks drawn up among the clouds with an angel as a teacher. No, maybe the angels would be monitors, and Jesus would be the teacher. On the other hand, Jesus would be too busy doing other things to take time teaching. It would be the Holy Spirit that would teach, he concluded. He remembered a verse somewhere about that. He prayed, "Jesus, I don't know what heaven will be like, and right now I don't really care. I do know that You have made it much better for me to live here on earth. I am very happy with it. Thank You." It was in that happy mood that he arrived at the ACTION office.

"Hello!" he said, sticking his head in. "Is Art here?"

"Yes, he is," one of the girls answered. "He will be out of his office in just a minute. He is talking to some men in there. My name is Corazon. What's yours?"

"Jaime. Jaime Jorka."

"Oh, yes. You have just been to camp and you are a very new Christian. Right?"

"How you know?" Jaime wondered.

Corazon tapped her forehead. "I know lots of things."

"You do?!" Jaime was completely taken.

"Of course! A good secretary knows everything her boss knows. Besides I just got through typing a list, and your name was on it." Her bright laugh washed away any resentment Jaime had at being fooled. "We keep track of all you fellows. We aren't going to leave you all alone now that you are members of our family."

"Family? What family?"

"God's family!" Art's voice boomed from the office door. He strode over to Jaime and gave him a big hug. Jaime hugged back openly and unashamedly. A surge of emotion went through him, and he laughed at the unaccustomed feeling of love. A picture of his own father went through his mind and cut the laughter short.

"I looked for you yesterday. We want to get a Bible study going. But your mother said you didn't live there anymore. What's up?"

"Oh, boy!" Jaime laughed. "You got a lot of time? It's a long story."

"We got time."

Jaime started with when he got off the bus and told of getting kicked out of home, learning to shine shoes, the robbery attempt, Rio's attack, the incident with the dog, and giving his shine box away. "So you see," he finished; "I learn what you try to tell me. I gotta depend on friend Jesus, not try to show Him how good I am. He wants to use me any way I am. Here's one peso. Now I only owe you two hundred ninety-nine."

"That's wonderful!" There was not a dry eye in the whole office. "Jaime, it's guys like you that make our work all worthwhile. But tell me, what are you going' to do now?"

"I don't know. But friend Jesus gonna take care of me."

"Yeah." Art was taken aback for a minute. Jaime's was a new and precious faith, and he was worried about it. There are not very many jobs for young boys these days, and Jaime needed something.

"Wait a minute! I wonder —" Art stuck his head in his office. "Hey, look who's out here," he called to those inside.

Out stepped Mr. Mendieta and Mr. Torre.

"Ah! Our little nail bender!" said Mr. Torre.

"Jaime! So good to see you." Mr. Mendieta grabbed his hand in a big, warm handshake. "How are you and Jesus getting along, huh?"

"Fine, fine. New things happening all the time." They laughed at his understatement.

"We had just hired the men for a new project we're starting," Art explained. "It's going to be a school to teach young fellows like yourself carpentry, car mechanics, metal work, and things like that. At least we hope it will." The uncertainty of mission finances rested heavily on Art. "We have a place in Cavite, and we are fixing it up with classrooms and stuff. These men are ready to start and I was wondering —"

The two men looked at each other. Mr. Torre shrugged. "Why not? We need somebody."

"Jaime, how would you like to work for us again?" Mr. Mendieta asked.

121

"You mean like before, where you teach me?"

"We teach you to be a carpenter so you can help build a place to learn to be a carpenter," Mr. Torre said.

"Sort of, only this time for pay." Mr. Mendieta was more serious.

"You give me *money?*"

"Some. We can't pay you very much."

"Yeah. We're pretty cheap carpenters," Mr. Torre threw in.

"How about eight pesos a day? You work for that?" It was below minimum wage.

"Eight pesos *every* day?" Jaime licked his lips at the thought of so much money.

"And we throw in lunch, too." Mr. Mendieta raised his eyebrows at Mr. Torte's offer. "My wife, she make it. It's only a few centavos more."

"Tondo is so far from Cavite, maybe we could find you a place to stay there when you work." Corazon was trying to be helpful.

"No!"

"You mean you don't want the job?"

"No — I mean yes — No, I do want the job. Yes, I will not stay in Cavite. That still isn't right, is it?" Jaime's mind raced as he thought over all the possibilities. They all waited for his answer.

"What I mean is I will take the job very much. Thank you for it. I start tomorrow?" The men nodded assent. "But I go home at night. It is far but I can take the bus. If I don't go home, who gonna tell my family how nice guy Jesus is? Others tell them and they not listen. But I go home with a job and I'm a big shot. They listen to me."

"But here's your chance to get out of Tondo. You could go back on weekends."

"I am out of Tondo. In my head I am out of there and in with Jesus. You know what I mean?"

A big grin spread over Art's face. "Yes, Jaime, I know very much what you mean."

"Now you see why I say friend Jesus take care of me." Jaime laughed with the pleasure of the thought. "Whether he have floppy ears like that dog or shined shoes like you. He take care of me." He hitched up his pants around his slight frame and headed for the door. "Now we see what happen next. Goodbye, people, see you tomorrow."

About the Author

Fletch Brown, since his salvation, has been a friend of missions. After becoming acquainted with missionaries from the Philippines and their work among street children, he gathered information and wrote *Street Boy.* The story is fiction, but it is based on real life experiences of underprivileged children in the Philippines.

What is ACTION?

ACTION is an interdenominational Christian organization whose purpose is to exercise and encourage evangelism, discipleship and development toward the fulfillment of the Great Commission of our Lord Jesus Christ (Matthew 28:18-20). As a missionary sending agency incorporated in Canada, Colombia, the Philippines, the United Kingdom, and the USA, ACTION also works with and assists national organizations in Brazil, Canada, Colombia, Ecuador, India, Mexico, New Zealand, the Philippines, and the Ukraine.

Our ministries include working with underprivileged and street children, as well as work with ethnic minorities, pastors and Christian workers, research and church development, mass media, literature production and distribution, community and social development, evangelism and dis-

124

cipleship, provision of staff for schools for missionary children, and administrative services for missionaries.

Dedicated career missionaries, short-term workers, and summer workers are used of the Lord to perform the ministries. Our need for more workers is pressing as opportunities abound in all areas of ministry in different countries and home offices.

ACTION is audited annually by an independent CPA, provides audited financial statements upon request, applies donated funds to the purposes for which they are raised, and carries on its business with the highest standards of integrity, avoiding conflicts of interest.

For more information contact:

ACTION USA
PO Box 398
Mountlake Terrace, WA 98043-0398
425-775-4800 • info@actionintl.org

ACTION Canada
PO Box 280
Three Hills, AB T0M 2A0
403-443-2211
ACTIONCanada@compuserve.com

ACTION UK
PO Box 694
Rhyl, Denbighshire, Wales LL18 1JU
actionuk@btinternet.com

ACTION Philippines
PO Box 14220
Ortigas Center
1605 Pasig City
PHILIPPINES
action@pacific.net.ph

ACTION New Zealand
PO Box 5263
Christchurch
crc@online.org
www.actionintl.org